Second Edition

SHADOW CHILDREN

Second Edition

SHADOW CHILDREN

Understanding Education's #1 Problem

Anthony Dallmann-Jones, Ph.D.
Professor, Educational Studies Division, Marian College
Director, National At-Risk Education Network (NAREN)

DEStech Publications, Inc.

Shadow Children, 2nd Edition

DEStech Publications, Inc.
439 North Duke Street
Lancaster, Pennsylvania 17602 U.S.A.

Printed in the United States of America
10 9 8 7 6 5 4 3

A RLD Publications book
Bibliography: p. 189
Index p. 201

ISBN: 978-0-9787610-3-5
Library of Congress Control Number: 2011927906

Dedications

The lost ones and their relentless rescuers

*In this second edition, a special thank you
to the Angel-Warrior Educators prepared
by the Marian University DIAL Program*

Table of Contents

Preface

EDUCATORS and parents: It is very important for me to speak with both of you. I have been observing teachers for over six decades both as a student and educator. As a therapist, educator *and* parent, I have observed the power of parents in children's lives. Most of the time I find teachers and parents admirable. Raising and educating children to be healthy yet diverse is courageous work. We all have our ups and downs, families and schools alike. It is easy to criticize. Too easy. It is inaccurate and hardly intelligent to judge ourselves based on what happens in snapshots of time.

What is of critical importance, however, is to be able to manifest the *willingness* to see things a bit differently. If we do just that, our behaviors will change automatically. It is not required that we work any harder than before, or spend any more money, or sacrifice anything—except our previous erroneous viewpoints. If we are but willing to take in a little new knowledge and let the implications of that knowledge take root, marvelous changes can occur. That is really the hurdle we must jump—yet how few do it. If we are not willing to see things differently the principle of education sits on a faulty foundation. To deliberately learn anything one must have the ability and the willingness to change.

Our society includes a large and increasing population of children slipping through the cracks. Shadow Children are the identifiably at risk and they come from all walks of life. They earn the title of Shadow Children because they are hiding—some quietly unnoticed, some obviously disregarded and dismissed, and some hidden in plain sight—the *real person* deep inside, and fear is its gatekeeper. Shadow Children, as such, often go unnoticed in their own homes and schools—until it is too late.

One purpose of this book is to reach out to you, the educators, and direct your attention to these children so they *can* be noticed, assessed, and helped. As a teacher, you may have students you suspect are discouraged about school and life. Perhaps you are reading this across the table from your child who is eating breakfast, and you wonder if something is amiss. The objective is not to surmise, but *know*. Why? Because we spawn and school our young population only to lose them. Along with such a loss comes indescribable pain and suffering.

The loss of a child comes in many forms. There is the obvious (suicide, alcohol, drugs, running away) and the not-so-obvious (compulsivity, mental illness, and spiritual diminishment). One of the most unrecognized, yet common, is this: *The failure to have a successful life.*

Eighteen years spent in a family and in schools is meant to prepare one for success in life. It is supposed to. If a family is strong and positive it can survive a weak educational system. If the school is strong and positive it can help a child overcome the effects of a dysfunctional family. But if the family *and* the school are ineffective at preparing a child for the rest of his or her life, we will always have prisons. Eighty-five percent of the prison space in the United States was created in the last 30 years (Spelman 2009). These prisons are filled with survivors of dysfunctional families and schools. There is a message here. Will anyone look for it? And if so, who will respond? Hence, this book.

The Numbers

The figures used in this book are interpretations and extrapolations from the 2000 Census, plus what is known as core data. Core data is information compiled throughout the 10-year interval between each census conducted by the U.S. Bureau of the Census.

The Condition of Education 2000–2008, a report compiled by the National Center for Education Statistics, part of the U.S. Department of Education, is derived from Common Core Data (CCD). Common Core Data is the Department of Education's primary database on public elementary and secondary education in the United States. It is a comprehensive statistical database that is updated yearly, containing information on all public elementary and secondary schools (approximately 94,000) and school districts (approximately 17,000) in the nation. Additionally, the data is designed to be comparable across all states.

Common Core Data includes the findings of five surveys that are completed annually by state education departments using their administrative records. Common Core Data includes a general description of each school and each school district, along with its name, address, and phone number. It contains data on students and staff, including demographics, as well as fiscal data, including revenues and current expenditures. As such, CCD offers the most reliable accumulation of information on the public school system of the United States.

Education Populations

The most current reported figures (2006–2007) tell us there are 49,644,937 students enrolled in public schools. There are approximately 1,500,000 home-schooled students. During the 2007 school year there were 28,996 private schools, enrolling a total of 6,066,520 students. While these numbers change daily, care has been taken to gather and compile the most up-to-date and accurate data. Examples of data gathering are included to illustrate the detailed process of arriving at cost figures. All that being said, *the real point is not the numbers, but what they signify.*

The President Speaks

During the George W. Bush administration a federal initiative was begun, No Child Left Behind (NCLB). For 7 years schools were—depending on your viewpoint—put on notice or encouraged to do something about the number of children whose needs were not being met at public schools. Whether due to new terminology, such as changing the definition of the word *dropout,* improved data gathering, or that NCLB was an ineffective program, in those 7 years the dropout figures more than doubled! (In the first edition of this book, published in 2006, I highlight a figure of approximately 500,000 dropouts per year.)

If those figures were seen as staggering by the Bush administration, I wonder how they are viewed by the Obama administration. Read on.

In an article on the subject (*Washington Post,* March 1, 2010), Michael Fletcher and Nick Anderson report on President Obama's strategy for schools.

President Obama outlined a get-tough strategy for turning around persistently struggling schools, offering an unprecedented increase in federal funding for local school systems that shake up their lowest-achieving campuses. Speaking before a meeting of America's Promise Alliance, an education group founded by former Secretary of State Colin Powell and his wife, Alma, Obama called curbing the nation's dropout rate a pressing economic and social imperative.

"This is a problem we cannot afford to accept and we cannot afford to ignore," President Obama said at the U.S. Chamber of Commerce headquarters. "The stakes are too high—for our children, for our economy and for our country."

According to a White House fact sheet, "Every school day, about 7,000 students decide to drop out of school—a total of 1.2 million students each year—and only about 70 percent of entering high school freshman graduate every year." As a result of this "dropout crisis," it said, the nation loses $319 billion a year in potential earnings.

The problem is concentrated in the nation's poorest schools and among minority students. Just 2,000 of America's schools—about 12 percent of the nation's total—account for half of the nation's dropouts, and more than 50 percent of them are African Americans or Latinos. Boys are also much more likely than girls to be unsuccessful in school.

President Obama has sought to combat the dropout problem with an infusion of federal aid for school districts that come up with innovative plans to help students graduate. The president's budget for the fiscal year that begins in October proposes $900 million for school turnaround grants, up from $546 million in fiscal 2010. The economic stimulus law enacted last year provided an additional $3 billion for the turnaround initiative. The 2011 budget, released last month, awaits action in Congress. . . .

With the proposed $900 million in school turnaround funding, President Obama is placing a bet on four strategies to fix thousands of schools in which reform ideas have come and gone without success.

Each of the strategies, at minimum, appears to require replacing the school's principal. The "turnaround" model would also require replacing at least half the school staff. "Restart" schools would be transferred to the control of independent charter networks or other school management organizations. "Transformation" schools would be required to take steps to raise teacher effectiveness and increase learning time, among other measures. The fourth strategy would be closing a school and dispersing its students.

Critics of school accountability programs say the suggested remedies are unproven and that the circumstances of struggling schools vary so significantly that uniform remedies would be ineffective in most cases.

This is a terrible way to start a book! Our figures are in disagreement, big time! And, if the reliability of the data is bad now, it is going to get worse. I recently completed the 2010 Census. The form contains only 10 questions, and no longer asks how many in the household have graduated, the last grade completed, or the income per person.

The 2000 Census appears to be the last one that we will have data about high school completion rates that are self reported, and come from the people themselves. Some say we will have better data because we will get it directly from the schools. I doubt it. My guess is that it will be worse (meaning more unreliable) because as schools are punished with firings and funding cuts for having high dropout rates, new means of fudging will find their way into statistical distortion. This became apparent as soon as NCLB was instituted.[1] When you pressure people with the loss of their jobs they will do whatever it takes to hold onto them, and also find a way to justify it.

[1]Former Secretary of Education Rod Paige, who served during the George W. Bush administration, was Houston's Superintendent of Schools before heading the U.S. Department of Education. Paige, who called the NEA a "terrorist organization," was appointed Secretary of Education based on his record of straightening out the school system "by holding principals accountable" and totally eliminating dropouts in Houston. In 2002 an Assistant Principal in Sharpstown, Texas admitted his school, which had reported zero dropouts, actually had 438 dropouts in that year. One year, one school: 438 dropouts, but reporting none. Then the truth came out across the system. All of the high schools had significant dropouts. Why was this not known? Principals had been ordered to find "legitimate ways" of explaining students who no longer attended. One technique, used by the front desk personnel who helped students to complete the necessary forms to formally drop out, was to coax students to indicate that they "might" pursue a GED at some time. Through a loophole in the policy, you were no longer considered a dropout if it was stated you would later pursue a GED. The count looked good. *Perfect,* as a matter of fact!

Acknowledgments

To my dear friends Jim and Jan Dallmann:
Who helped prepare this book for my editing.
(I apologize, I really did not know it would take that long!)

To my dear wife and beloved partner, Amy:
I asked you to "Make my day" and you made my nights as well.

To my publisher, Richard Dunn, of RLD Publications:
Who believes in my works enough to publish them—no small undertaking.

And lastly, to the Abused & Neglected Children:
I wish you two special things: (1) The courage to overcome that which you
did not ask for and, (2) an Angel/Warrior Educator who cares about you.

Introduction

I grabbed Bob's arm before he could slam his fist angrily onto the table again. The judge looked at us, a scowl spreading across his face, replacing the deadpan look that most judges seem to wear. It did not silence Bob in the least.

"That's lame!" he exclaimed, his face reddening "That is so damn lame!"

My mind filled with the vision of calling my wife from jail. "Honey, I can't dine with your parents tonight because I am having collards and corn bread with the fellas—in our little cell."

Even the hardened social worker, who had probably dealt with almost every sordid form of abuse that the rest of us don't even want to know about, jumped.

Bob was undaunted. "Judge, you just *cannot* send Lydia back into that home, for Chrissakes!"

Lucky for Bob, Judge Seymour was a juvenile judge familiar with such outbursts, though usually from teenagers. Lucky for both of us we were not in his courtroom, where contempt charges often accompanied such uncontrolled behavior.

"Calm down, Robert." Judge Seymour's face softened. "I appreciate what you're attempting to do, I really do. But, frankly, there's not much that I can do."

I took a deep breath. Ann Bennett, the Tallahassee social worker, cleared her throat, straightened her skirt, and took an obvious deep breath, lessening her tension.

Bob, however, was not finished. "Well, this just bites! This kid comes into my class the day after Christmas vacation with scabs on her back the size of giant leeches after her drunken dad—if you can call him that—beat her half to death for a very Merry Christmas morning. You're going to put her back in that war zone? Holy crap, Judge!"

The judge's scowl was back. Ann stiffened again. I could smell the fatback cooking. I put my hand on top of Bob's arm and quickly interceded. "Please understand, Judge, this little girl was beaten, not only for something she didn't do, but she also received no medical attention. And then, she had to sleep on a single mattress, on the floor, with her younger brothers and sisters for the next week until she came back to school and the nurse could treat her."

I look back and realize how naive I was. Not only about the struggles of dysfunctional family survivor children at school, but about what a truly caring teacher looked like. I was 28 years old, serving my administrative internship in an elementary school as part of my graduate studies at Florida State University. Bob and I had become friends. I admired him because he was a champion for have-nothing kids. At his own expense he stocked a small variety store in the supply room adjoining his sixth-grade classroom. He bought combs, toothbrushes, tooth paste, healthy snacks, clothes, soap, barrettes, and all kinds of little goodies for 11 year olds. He made an arrangement with the nurse to take certain at-risk kids down to the shower in her office where she would get them all cleaned up for the day. If the kids took their showers, brushed their teeth, combed their hair, they could pick something out of Bob's store. He was always making home visits to check up on "his kids." He bought things for them with his own money, and did whatever he could to help them have a better chance at a good sixth-grade year.

His classroom was a whirlwind of activity centers, filled with laughter and high-energy learning. Bob had designed and implemented a program that established the first Youth Tutoring Youth (YTY) program in Leon County, whereby unmotivated, unsuccessful sixth-grade readers spent an hour a day teaching first-graders beginning reading. They also made picture dictionaries together. Bob was always doing innovative and kid-centered things like that.

Lydia was a major and very special project of Bob's. Her family was highly dysfunctional. Lydia's mother worked in a Florida tung nut orchard. Tung nuts are a major ingredient in oil-based paints, varnishes, and shellacs. They are still grown and harvested on plantation-like farms in Southern states, particularly Florida, Alabama, and Mississippi. Though chestnut-like in appearance, they are highly toxic, as many unfortunates have discovered. Ingesting the flesh of a tung nut will likely hospitalize you with severe, flu-like symptoms. A horticultural reference to the tung nut includes the following, exclamation point and all: Highly Toxic, May Be Fatal If Eaten!"

Lydia's mother worked with a group of African American women who moved quickly ahead of the tung nut harvesting machines, picking up loose material, branches, and sticks to prevent them from going into the machine. If the women moved too slowly they were prodded or, I was told, even whipped with sticks by white foremen. Lydia's mother had picked up sticks for 20 years, and seemed permanently stooped over as a result.

Lydia's biological father worked in a lumber mill during the day and apparently drank every night after work. It seemed he loved to beat people, especially helpless people like his wife and his children. The only time I spoke with him I was sure he was brain damaged. Their eldest daughter, Lydia, was becoming damaged in her own way. I began to think that as a result of the abuse done to her she was aphasic, as neither Bob nor I had heard her speak.

The school records were unclear as to how old she was. She was a relatively tall girl for a sixth-grader. She wore her hair in little gathered sprigs, knotted together with twine by her mother. She had beautiful, chestnut-colored eyes; large and wide in seeming apprehension. I had seen her eyes only once, as she seemed reluctant to lift them to make eye contact. Bob was trying to rescue Lydia. She often came to school filthy and had (we discovered later) almost every intestinal parasite common to Florida, including the roundworm Ascaris, tape worm, and tiny nocturnal parasites known as pinworms that make your anus itch all night long as they crawl in and out to lay eggs.

A visit by Ann the social worker to Lydia's home, made on Bob's recommendation after *his* first visit, revealed that the family had no running water, a broken refrigerator, and a propane stove that was no longer functional. (This explained the piled boxes of rotting, unused, federally provided beans and rice on the sagging front porch.) Ann also reported that there was no toilet facility, not even an outhouse, and the family relieved themselves in the woods, over logs, and uphill of their well.

Bob had worked diligently to rid Lydia of lice. Slowly he helped her begin to take pride in her appearance. She showered, brushed her teeth, and combed her hair each morning, assisted by Nurse Green at the school clinic. Lydia was making good progress and had started, after 3 months, to begin smiling again. At a Christmas party on the last day before vacation break, Bob gave Lydia a dozen oranges to take home to her family for the holidays. According to the social worker's report, when Lydia got home that evening her mother lined the oranges up on a rafter in the living room, their only room, to be saved for Christmas Day, which was a few days later.

The next day was a work day but not a school day. Lydia, being the eldest, was the designated babysitter for all eight of her brothers and sisters while the parents went off to work. Over her frantic protests, a couple of Lydia's younger brothers took down the oranges and, sharing them with the smaller children, ate them all. Lydia refused to eat any of the oranges, knowing there was going to be hell to pay. The boys probably knew this as well, but hunger quickly drives out reason and trumps fear.

We learned from her brothers that when the father came home drunk on Christmas morning and was told by the mother what had happened, the father grabbed a piece of fan belt he used to punish his wife and children, took Lydia into the front yard and beat her across the back until she fainted. She was then sent to bed with no dinner and received nothing to eat for several days. Eight days later when Lydia returned to school, the horrified nurse, seeing the scabs on Lydia's back—many of them over four inches long and a half inch wide—called the authorities.

The parents now sat in the courtroom, nervously waiting to see what the white judge was going to do to the poor black folks. The judge had taken one look at the papers, the pictures, the charges, and the pathetic sniveling parents, and had called Bob, myself, and the school social worker into his chambers.

Judge Seymour sat behind his desk, stacked the papers, squared the edges, then looked at Bob. "Robert, don't think I'm not going to put the fear of God into them. I am going to scare the hell out of them, but . . ."

Bob stared back. "But what?"

I cringed, definitely feeling Bob was edging towards his breaking point. Secretly, of course, I admired his willingness to risk arguing with a judge. But I realized it was probably useless, and this became apparent as the judge continued.

"Robert," he said, nodding at us, "Tony, Ann. Face it. First of all, the foster homes in Tallahassee are full. And secondly," he lowered his voice, "who is going to take in a poor, black, speechless, sixth-grader in *this* town?"

It went downhill from there as was indicated by the rest of the hearing. The judge threatened the parents. The mother cried repeatedly, "Don't take my baby from me!" The father just hung and shook his scarred, shaved head and acted repentant for what he couldn't even remember doing.

Then Lydia went home with her parents.

Similar stories like this are repeated in America many times daily. Worse, these are only the abused and neglected children that come to light. *How many stay in the shadows?* It is tragic how many. But *it is real!* Especially for the children who live in them.

Every day in America:[2]

- 4 children are killed by abuse or neglect.
- 1 young person dies from HIV infection.
- 5 children or teens commit suicide.
- 9 children or teens are killed by firearms.
- 202 children are arrested for violent crimes (up from 155 the previous year).
- 377 children are arrested for drug abuse (up from 296 the previous year).
- 2,175 children are confirmed as abused or neglected.
- 4,498 babies are born to unmarried mothers (up from 4,017 the previous year).
- 1,210 babies are born to teen mothers.
- 2,483 babies are born into poverty (up from 2,411 the previous year).
- 2,222 children drop out of high school every school day (1 of every 4 high school freshmen fails to finish high school in 4 years in the United States.).
- 4,435 children are arrested (up from 3,477 the previous year).
- 18,493 public school students are suspended every school day (up from 18,221 the previous year).

This is every day, or every school day! Multiply these figures by 365 (or for school days, 180)—if you can bear it.

Q: Can children, enduring the suffering implied by these statistics, succeed in school?

A: Not very well, and certainly not if the school system is insensitive and non-supportive and has no compensatory programs in place. Here are some additional, staggering figures.

[2]*Source:* Children's Defense Fund 2010a.

In the United States:

- 9,200,000 children are without health insurance (U.S. Bureau of the Census 2008).
- 19 percent of America's children live in poverty. Correspondingly, the number of children living in families with incomes below the official poverty line was predicted to rise from a low of 12.3 million in 2006 to about 14.1 million in 2010—an increase of 1.8 million (U.S. Bureau of the Census 2008). Sadly, this estimate became reality 2 years earlier than expected. In 2008 the United States had 14.1 million children living in families below the official poverty line (Federal Interagency Forum on Child and Family Statistics 2010). The 2010 figures of 43.6 million people (including the 14.1 million children) represent the highest numbers ever collected by the U.S. Bureau of the Census. This poverty rate is 14.3 percent of the U.S. population—roughly one in every seven adults.[3]

Q: Can children who have little or no health care and/or live in poverty succeed in school?

A: Not very well, and certainly not if the school system is insensitive, non-supportive, and has no compensatory programs in place. Or worse, if it re-victimizes the victims:

- 1,240 public school students are corporally punished every school day (Children's Defense Fund 2010a).

It seems everyone has a different set of numbers. The data fluctuates and definitions are inconsistent. What is a dropout? For that matter, what is a graduate? The American Youth Policy Forum is a non-profit organization that accumulates research data in Washington, DC and has significant influence on American educational policy. Here are excerpts from their research-based report, *By the Numbers: Every Nine Seconds in America a Student Becomes a Dropout* (2005).

- Among the incarcerated, 75 percent of those in state prison and 59 percent of those in federal prison are high school dropouts.

---

[3]In this book you will see three different references to poverty levels. They are obviously not quoting from each other, showing independent and more reliable data gathering. In the end, however, no matter which one on any given day is accurate, the numbers are particularly horrible at this time in our civilization.

- High school dropouts are 3.5 times more likely than graduates to be incarcerated.
- Dropouts contribute disproportionately to the unemployment rate. In 2001, 55 percent of young adult dropouts were employed, compared to 74 percent of high school graduates and 87 percent of college graduates.
- Dropouts contribute to state and federal tax coffers at about one-half the rate of high school graduates. Over a working lifetime, a dropout will contribute about $60,000 less.
- The 23 million high school dropouts aged 18–67 will contribute roughly $50 billion less annually in state and federal taxes.
- Studies suggest the United States would save $41.8 billion in health care costs if the 600,000 young people who dropped out in 2004 were to complete 1 additional year of education.
- If 33 percent of dropouts graduated from high school, the federal government would save $10.8 billion each year in food stamps, housing assistance, and temporary assistance for needy families.
- Testifying before Congress, Secretary of Education Margaret Spellings said dropouts cost the United States "more than $260 billion . . . in lost wages, lost taxes and lost productivity over their lifetimes."

CHAPTER 1

Who Are Shadow Children?

We are in an educational war on the home front.
We must wake up, arm ourselves,
and unite in the effort to save the young people of our country.

ONE of the goals of this book is to make the invisible visible, to bring into awareness that which we were previously unaware of, to bring into the foreground what was formerly background, to bring into the light those in the shadows. These are Shadow Children, the *at-risk children*. They are often easy to miss, easy to ignore, and yet desperately need to be seen and serviced. The cost of continuing to ignore this problem will stagger you.

There is serious debate over exactly what the term *at risk* means. Some deny there is a need for such a term. We will examine this denial and the cover-ups that exist and why they happen.

The National At-Risk Education Network (NAREN), a non-profit organization founded in 2000 that is dedicated solely to studying this critical issue and supporting the educators who work on behalf of Shadow Children, has a two-pronged definition for the term *at-risk youth:*

1. At risk of dropping out of school
2. At risk of not succeeding in life because of unfavorable circumstances

Sometimes a student falls into both categories, but all Shadow Children fall into at least one. Schools need to be ready to support children in either category.

How Can the Tide Be Turned?

When you are a Shadow Child, you feel the price tag every single day. You feel it as a deficit in various parts of your being: your

1

emotions, your finances, your health, your relationships, your spirit, your limited opportunities, your thought processes—any or all of these. You don't need any convincing that the "cost" of being a Shadow Child is too high. As an adult, if you are still paying the price(s), you will usually not be able to improve your lot in life until you realize this *one critical fact:*

> *I may not be responsible for what happened to me as a child but, fair or not, I am 100% responsible for my own recovery.*

You cannot rehab someone—only they can do it. But, when needed, a supporting role is not necessarily as passive as it sounds. While children must take some responsibility, even by just exhibiting a willingness to get better, knowledgeable adults who understand that all children are *our* children should take responsibility for matching up a child's needs with the appropriate services or programs to assist the child in recovering enough to have a successful life. This supporting role is often filled by educators who know enough to suggest to parents directly that their children receive the proper services. If there is no response from the familial caregivers, there are more formal channels within the educator's administration that can be utilized to get children the help they need. The important thing is to *do something,* not just look the other way or trust it to fate.

The concept of school has changed. *The goal of school is success, and not just succeeding at school work but also succeeding at life in general.* Many savvy educators have seen that often there is too much "static" in the head of an abused/neglected/traumatized child to absorb new content. Until the extent of the static is minimized, the ability of the child to learn is commensurately limited. In other words, it is proportional: the more abuse, neglect, or trauma a child has internalized, the more recovery work is needed. There are professionals who do this work with children to overcome their past, just like there are counselors for adults. Supporting someone who is trying to recover is a noble effort.

Individually, the efforts and costs of recovery are unique and not always external. They may involve quantities in life such as money and possessions. More often, for the survivor, the personal issues are about qualities of life: meaningfulness, fulfillment, vitality, relationships, and that mysterious thing called happiness. Each Shadow Child has a story worthy of study, and each Shadow Child is worth the effort it takes for remediation. However, to intervene on a larger community, state, or even national scale will take a different kind of awareness. To remedy the mechanisms in our society that (1) create a Shadow Child population and (2) fail to rehabilitate the Shadow Child population once it has been created, we need to create powerful campaigns of reform. There are three equally valid approaches to directly impact people with these campaigns.

Arousing Injustice

The first valid approach is appealing to a sense of *injustice:* "These poor children! It's not fair! No kid asked to be placed at risk!" If you have been a Shadow Child, this approach usually grabs you at some point, at least for a while. You know what it is like to be kicked while down or have no one healthy mentoring you and there for you when you need them. You know what it is like to be shunned, shamed, abused, neglected, or to live a life of restriction in poverty. Oprah Winfrey comes to mind as a role model. She has admitted her childhood anguish on television, and you can easily discern her deep feelings for the downtrodden because of it. Her role in *The Color Purple* is a tribute to her desire for encouraging others to use their anger to rise above the abuse and live a good life. Campaigns touting the injustices befalling Shadow Children will reach certain segments of the population who have been there and move them to action.

Creating Compassion

The second valid campaign approach is via *compassion.* If you are a person of unusual compassion you have a tender heart, the ability to empathize, and a willingness to believe and respect others' experiences without having to experience them yourself. Princess Diana and her work with children with AIDS comes to mind. Has there ever been a more impassioned speech than hers at an AIDS Conference in Edinburgh in September of 1993? In part, she stated:

> And what of the children who live with HIV every day? Not because they're necessarily ill themselves, but because their family life includes a mother, father, brother or sister who has the virus. How will we help

them come to terms with the loss of the people they love? How will we help them to grieve? How will we help them to feel secure about their future?

These children need to feel the same things as other children: To play, to laugh and cry, to make friends, to enjoy the ordinary experiences of childhood. To feel loved and nurtured and included by the world they live in, without the stigma that AIDS continues to attract. By listening to their needs, really listening, perhaps we can find the best way of helping these children to face their future with greater confidence and hope.

Princess Diana never had AIDS. How could she tap into those issues so well? Compassion, insight, openness to the experiences of others and humanitarian concern seemed to emanate from her. Compassionate campaigns will reach certain population segments enough to move them to proactive contributions of energy and resources to help bring about a remedy.

Appealing to the Intellect

The third valid approach is through *reason*. The best vehicle for this approach is often looking at the efficiency and money issues of the problem(s) created by having a population of Shadow Children. We will go into this issue at length as it is a complex one. Further, it is likely to be the approach that works with most legislators, power brokers, and others of significant influence in the business community.

What Is the Cost of Having a Population of Shadow Children?

Few people realize the financial aspects of having a population of Shadow Children (who grow into adults and often raise more Shadow Children). The reader may be quite unpleasantly surprised at the gigantic price tag for not doing something about this crisis—not just on the personal level, but also in the economic arena. Hopefully, the following data will be used to leverage (justify) more realistic expenditures for prevention and intervention programs in the future because basically the message is going to be: *You can pay now, or pay a whole lot more later.*[4]

The Cost of Child Abuse and Neglect

We shall look at several cost factors in the Shadow Child arena in the next chapter. Information for much of this section was provided with permission from the National Clearinghouse on Child Abuse and Neglect (NCCAN). This agency is now part of the U.S. Department of Health and Human Services and is called the Child Welfare Information Gateway. (It can be found online at www.childwelfare.gov.)

There is no better place to start than with the incredible cost of child abuse and neglect. Almost every Shadow Child became that way because of child abuse and neglect in some form. Child abuse and neglect cost our society dearly, not only in terms of the trauma caused to the maltreated individuals, but also in economic terms. Economic costs include the funds spent each year on child welfare services for abused and neglected children, as well as the large sums dedicated to addressing the short-term and long-term consequences of abuse and neglect. Effective prevention programs that promote the safety and well-being of children and families hold potential for lessening the suffering and trauma experienced by children and for greatly reducing these economic costs.

To date, few in-depth and rigorous financial analyses have been

[4]Teaching at nights in a medium security prison, I asked an administrator to see if he could find any prisoners in my class who came from just healthy, regular families. He couldn't find one.

A graduate student of mine was a support person at a mental health facility in the Green Bay area with patients who would probably never leave the facility. As he was a student in my course, Understanding At-Risk Children (a course that can be taken online through Marian University), I asked him if he would mind perusing the records of the 38 patients he worked with, to see how many came from abusive/neglectful homes. At the time we had class on campus. At the third class, he pulled me aside at break time. "Remember you asked me to check patient records to see how many came from abusive homes?"

"Yes, sure," I replied. "I am glad you did, or did you?"

"You bet I did." His eyes widened, "Dr. Dallmann-Jones, they *all* did! I was shocked! I still am."

I wasn't. I'm not. In this country, our prisons and mental health facilities are packed full of the end product of abusive and neglectful homes. Over 80 percent of the prisons in the United States have been built in the last 30 years (Spelman 2009).

Point made?

conducted to give us a solid understanding of the total costs of child maltreatment (i.e., the costs of not preventing child abuse and neglect), as compared to the economic savings associated with prevention. Nevertheless, several prevention advocates, researchers, and evaluators have begun to grapple with the research. We begin with a discussion of the cost elements that make up the total cost of child maltreatment. The next chapter highlights findings from selected studies that have conducted cost-benefit and cost-of-failure analyses.

There is a conspiracy in this country to protect parents more than their children. —Terry Kellogg, author *Broken Toys, Broken Dreams*

CHAPTER 2

Child Maltreatment Costs

*We educators will someday realize that where we once were
going forward, we missed a critical and humane aperture
to the future and in so doing began to reverse course,
now working strenuously to turn gold into lead.*

CHILD abuse and neglect have caused detrimental effects to the
physical, psychological, cognitive, and behavioral development of
children (Administration for Children and Families 2008). These
consequences range from minor to severe, and include physical injuries,
brain damage, chronic low self-esteem, problems with bonding and
forming relationships, developmental delays, learning disorders, and
aggressive behavior. Clinical conditions associated with abuse and neglect
include depression, post-traumatic stress disorder, and conduct disorders.

Beyond the trauma inflicted on individual children, child maltreatment
also has been linked with long-term, negative societal consequences. For
example, studies associate child maltreatment with increased risk of low
academic achievement, drug use, teen pregnancy, juvenile delinquency,
and adult criminality (Watts-English et al. 2006, Springer et al. 2007).

Further, these consequences cost society by expanding the need for
mental health and substance abuse treatment programs, police and court
interventions, correctional facilities, and public assistance programs in
addition to causing monumental losses in productivity. Calculation of
the total financial cost of child maltreatment must account for both the
direct costs and the indirect costs of its long-term consequences.

Direct Costs

Direct costs reflect expenditures incurred by the child welfare system
as well as the judicial, law enforcement, health care, and mental health

7

systems in responding to abused and neglected children and their families. Direct costs include expenses associated with hospitalization and medical services provided to treat injuries resulting from abuse; child protective services (CPS) and/or police investigations; foster care and other out-of-home placement services for maltreated children; and family preservation, rehabilitation, and treatment programs.

Government expenditures for child welfare programs provide a benchmark for estimating a portion of the annual direct costs of child abuse and neglect. For fiscal year 2006, federal expenditures to states for major child welfare programs exceeded $12 billion. This was equaled by state and local expenditures to bring the total to over $25 billion. This figure includes child welfare services, foster care, adoption assistance, and family preservation and support but excludes Medicaid dollars, an important source of treatment funding for children and families. Based on a survey of state child welfare agencies (Child Welfare League of America 2007), federal funding accounts for less than half (42%) of state child welfare expenditures with the remainder supported by state (49%) and local (9%) funding.

A study by the Missouri Children's Trust Fund (1997) provides a different lens through which to cost maltreatment. The study analyzed the direct economic costs of one type of child maltreatment, shaken baby syndrome (SBS), in Missouri over a 10-year period. The study found that the state spent at least $6.9 million, or approximately $32,500 on each of the 214 identified SBS victims. These costs included $4 million in Medicaid expenses, $1.9 million for Division of Family Services expenditures, and nearly $1 million for Department of Mental Health services.

Indirect Costs

Indirect costs reflect the long-term economic consequences of child maltreatment in such areas as special education, mental health, substance abuse, teen pregnancy, welfare dependency, domestic violence, homelessness, juvenile delinquency, and adult criminality. Indirect costs are more difficult to assess than direct costs, and frequently, calculations are based on assumptions, or they are extrapolated from research. Deborah Daro (1988), for example, estimated a national indirect juvenile delinquency cost of $14.9 million based on the following: an estimated 177,300 adolescent maltreatment victims nationwide in 1983; research indicating a 20 percent delinquency rate among adolescent victims; and average costs ($21,000 per year) for 2 years of correctional institutionalization for these abused and delinquent youth. The same analysis estimated that, if 1 percent of severely abused children were to suffer permanent disabilities, the annual cost of community services for treating children with developmental disabilities would increase by $1.1 million. (These figures would be much higher today.)

Indirect costs also may include inferred costs of lost productivity associated with injury, incarceration, long-term unemployment, or death. Daro's cost analysis, for example, projected the national cost in future lost productivity of severely abused or neglected children to be between $658 million and $1.3 billion each year, assuming that their impairments reduce their future earnings by as little as 5–10 percent. A Michigan study (Caldwell 1992) used rates of per capita income and average lifetime participation in the labor force to generate average lifetime earnings of, and calculate lost tax revenue from, those children who died as a result of child abuse or preventable infant mortality. The study concluded that, in addition to the devastating personal losses experienced by the families of the infants and children who died, the state lost an estimated $46 million in tax revenue. (Although this figure represents the loss of tax revenue over a lifetime, it can also be interpreted as the per year loss to the state if the rates of tax, abuse, and mortality remain relatively stable.)

As the above examples show, the total financial costs of child abuse and neglect can be quite high. Conversely, the potential benefits or savings from prevention also are high. These costs and potential savings form the basis of cost-benefit analyses.

Prevention Cost-Benefit Analyses

Few in-depth economic analyses have been conducted to assess the cost-effectiveness of child abuse prevention. Four key studies, presented below, compare the costs of preventive family support services with the savings generated from the positive outcomes of prevention programs and/or the direct and indirect costs of not preventing child maltreatment. Many prevention programs, including those referenced in the studies below, address not only prevention of child abuse and neglect, but also prevention of other threats to child and family well-being. Examples of such threats include preventable health conditions (e.g., low birth weight, infant mortality, newborn addictions), lack of economic self-sufficiency, social isolation, lack of parenting skills or knowledge, and inappropriate child-rearing behaviors. Several of these other threats also represent precursors or risk factors associated with abuse and neglect. As such, the benefits generated by addressing these risk factors are included in this broad view of the costs related to child maltreatment.

Case Studies

The National Clearinghouse on Child Abuse and Neglect (NCCAN) provides four case studies to illustrate how costing is computed in various scenarios. The studies included are older, but the point is to give the reader some insight into the reasoning behind the twists and turns of gathering accurate data in a complex and convoluted financial situation in conjunction with an equally complex set of human circumstances.

Elmira, New York

A report by David Olds and colleagues presents an economic analysis within a rigorous evaluation based on a randomized trial of a nurse home visitation program serving 400 pregnant women in Elmira, New York. The evaluation indicated that frequent home visits by nurses during pregnancy and the first 2 years of the child's life improved a wide range of maternal and child health outcomes among adolescent, unmarried, and low-income, first-time mothers (Olds et al. 1993).

The study found that, in contrast to women assigned to the comparison group, nurse-visited women experienced: (1) improved health-related behaviors (e.g., reduced cigarette use and improved diets) and use of prenatal services during pregnancy, (2) fewer emergency room visits for children during the second year of life, (3) greater workforce participation, and (4) fewer subsequent pregnancies for low-income and unmarried women. In addition, among poor, unmarried teenage women, the study observed a 75 percent reduction in state-verified cases of child abuse and neglect during the first 2 years of a child's life.

The economic analysis for the Elmira home visitation program concluded that government savings could offset the program costs for low-income participants within 4 years (Olds et al. 1993). The analysis estimated an average cost of $3,133 per family (1980 dollars) for providing home visitation services to low-income participants, based on expenditures for nurses' salaries, benefits, supplies, and transportation. These costs were compared with reduced expenditures in other government programs affected by the positive outcomes of home visitation. The economic impact of improved maternal and child functioning was evaluated from a standpoint of four government programs—Aid to Families with Dependent Children (AFDC), Medicaid, Food Stamps, and Child Protective Services (CPS)—as well as increased tax revenues generated by subsequent employment.

Within low-income families, for the 4-year period following the child's birth, the estimated per family government savings was $3,498 (Olds et al. 1993). The majority of estimated government savings (based on comparison group expenditures) was derived from reductions in AFDC and food stamp payments, which were associated with increased employment and reduced subsequent pregnancies among program clients.

Michigan

A 1992 study for the Michigan Children's Trust Fund (Caldwell 1992) concluded that providing either comprehensive parent education or home visitation service for every Michigan family expecting its first child would amount to only 5 percent of the estimated total state cost of maltreatment. Based on an estimated per-family cost of $712, statewide prevention services were projected at approximately $43 million. In comparison, analysts figured that child maltreatment and inadequate prenatal care cost the state approximately $823 million. Michigan's total estimated annual cost of child maltreatment and inadequate prenatal care included direct and indirect costs associated with the following:

- protective services ($38 million)
- foster care ($74 million)
- health costs of low birth-weight babies ($256 million)
- medical treatment of injuries caused by abuse ($5 million)
- special education costs ($6 million)
- psychological care for child maltreatment victims ($16 million)
- juvenile justice system and correction services ($207 million)
- adult criminality ($175 million)
- projected tax revenue lost from infant deaths ($46 million)

In making these estimates, a series of extrapolations were used to account for the proportion of total spending that can be linked to maltreatment. For example, prior research (Loeber and Stouthamer-Loeber 1987) suggests that approximately 20 percent of children from abusive homes commit delinquent acts as juveniles, and 25 percent of these go on to commit crimes as adults. Based on these findings, the Michigan researchers predicted that, of the 39,452 children identified as abused that year, 1,996 would become involved in the adult criminal justice system. With an average annual state adult prison cost of $25,000, and an average prison sentence of 3.5 years, total adult criminality associated with child abuse and neglect was estimated to cost $175 million (1,996 × $25,000 × 3.5).

Colorado

A similar 1995 analysis, commissioned by the Colorado Children's Trust Fund, examined the costs incurred in the state of Colorado by failing to prevent child abuse and neglect and then compared these costs with the savings that would accrue from an investment in effective prevention services (Gould and O'Brien 1995). The state estimated $190 million in annual direct costs for child maltreatment, including the costs of CPS investigations, child welfare services to children in their own homes, and out-of-home placements. In addition, annual indirect costs were calculated based on an assumption that $212 million (approximately 20 percent of the $1 billion total expenditure) in state social programs were associated with the long-term consequences to individuals maltreated as children (e.g., special education, AFDC assistance payments, job training programs, youth institutional and community programs, mental health programs for children and adults, substance and drug abuse programs, victim services, criminal justice programs, domestic violence shelters, and prisons). Indirect costs ($212 million) and direct costs ($190 million) combined for an estimated total of $402 million in annual expenditures related to abuse and neglect.

The state costs of maltreatment were compared to the potential savings associated with an intensive home visitor prevention program targeted toward those families most at risk of abuse and neglect. Based on an estimated $2,000 per-family cost of a statewide home visitation program for high-risk families with children from birth to 3 years old, the Colorado analysis projected total costs of $32 million. At the time of the study, $8 million was being spent in the state on home visitation and family support, thus suggesting a need for $24 million in new money. The Colorado analysis concluded that, if the program were able to reduce child maltreatment expenditure by only 6 percent (0.06 × $402 million annual expenditure), the cost of the prevention investment would be offset.

Allegheny County, Pennsylvania

Bruner (1996) used statistical modeling to estimate benefits or savings as the potential returns on investment from family centers for high-risk neighborhoods in Allegheny County, Pennsylvania. This study approaches the *cost of failure* by contrasting the level of spending on remediation, maintenance, and CPS for residents living in the highest risk, distressed neighborhoods of the county with the level of spending in lower risk neighborhoods in the same county. This approach captures real-world comparisons for estimates of "what could be."

The study first determined the potential savings obtainable by transforming the high-risk neighborhoods into neighborhoods similar to the rest of Allegheny County. This potential savings, or cost of failure, included expenditures across a number of public spending areas most associated with preventable maltreatment and health problems in childhood: AFDC, Medicaid, food stamps, children and youth social services, juvenile justice, jail and prison, and lost economic activity and tax revenue. The analysis concluded that the county would save approximately $565 million annually in public spending, or $416.3 million, if these costs were discounted over a 20-year timeframe.

Costs were calculated for establishing family centers to serve populations within the high-risk neighborhoods. This analysis was grounded in the existing body of research on the various elements needed for children to succeed, the principles of effective frontline practice, and the potential long-term effects of such strategies upon child outcomes. The study projected that serving 45–60 percent of all families with very young children in Allegheny County high-risk neighborhoods would require an expansion of funding of $11.9 million, from $6.6 million (for existing centers with a capacity for 2,640 families) to $18.5 million (to serve up to 8,400 families).

From a return-on-investment perspective, the $18.5 million expenditure can be compared with the $416.3 million estimated long-term preventable expenditures. An $18.5 million investment would have to contribute to reducing such preventable financial costs by only 5 percent for it to be considered cost-effective.

Conclusion

In each of the above studies, the analysts concluded that the positive outcomes of prevention programs, with even relatively small reductions in the rate of child maltreatment, demonstrate that prevention can be cost-effective. Although much remains to be learned about the optimal levels of investment in prevention, these studies present a starting point for continued analysis and discussion.

To estimate the financial costs of the long-term consequences of child maltreatment on adolescent and adult development and behavior, cost-benefit analyses must take a holistic and long-term perspective. Most of the investments in prevention, particularly as they apply to investments in families with young children, are likely to have "payback curves" that extend over a long period of time, with much of the savings occurring when the child reaches a healthy, productive, and nonviolent adulthood (Bruner and Scott 1994). While additional investment, research, careful documentation, and well-designed analysis is needed within the prevention field—both to assess the effectiveness of prevention programs and its cost-effectiveness—current findings suggest that, over the long term, *prevention pays.*

In 2001, funded by a grant from the Edna McConnell Clark Foundation, Prevent Child Abuse America conducted a study using conservative estimates, meaning those standards set down by the U.S. Department of Health and Human Services' Harm Standard, the most stringent classification category. In addition, they did not attempt to quantify *all* indirect costs of abuse and neglect, including the provision of welfare benefits to adults whose economic condition is a direct result of abuse and neglect. Even with this conservative estimating the figure came out to *$94,000,000,000* a year!

This is how this figure was computed:

DIRECT COSTS

Statistical Justification Data

Hospitalization

Rationale: 565,000 children were reported as suffering serious harm from abuse in 1993. One of the less severe injuries is a broken or fractured bone. Cost of treating a fracture or dislocation of the radius or ulna, per incident, is $10,983.

Calculation: 565,000 × $10,983
$6,205,395,000

Chronic Health Problems

Rationale: 30 percent of maltreated children suffer chronic medical problems. The cost of treating a child with asthma, per incident, in the hospital is $6,410.

Calculations: 0.30 × 1,553,800 = 446,140; 446,140 × $6,410
$2,987,957,400

Mental Health Care System

Rationale: 743,200 children were abused in 1993. For purposes of obtaining a conservative estimate, neglected children are not included. One of the costs to the mental health care system is counseling. Estimated cost per family for counseling is $2,860. One in five abused children is estimated to receive these services.

Calculations: 743,200/5 = 148,640; 148,640 × $2,860
$425,110,400

Child Welfare System

Rationale: The Urban Institute published a paper in 1999 with the results of a study it conducted that estimated child welfare costs associated with child abuse and neglect to be $14.4 billion.
$14,400,000,000

Law Enforcement

Rationale: The National Institute of Justice estimates the following costs of police services for each of the following interventions: child sexual abuse ($56), physical abuse ($20), emotional abuse ($20), and child educational neglect ($27). These numbers were cross-referenced against U.S. Department of Health and Human Services statistics on the number of incidences occurring annually.

Calculations: Physical Abuse—381,700 × $20 = $7,634,000; Sexual Abuse—217,700 × $56 = $12,191,200; Emotional Abuse—204,500 × $20 = $4,090,000; and Educational Neglect—397,300 × $2 = $794,600
$24,709,800

Judicial System

Rationale: The Dallas Commission on Children and Youth determined the cost per initiated court action for each case of child maltreatment was $1,372.34. Approximately 16 percent of child abuse victims have court action taken on their behalf.

Calculations: 1,553,800 cases nationwide × 0.16 = 248,608 victims with court action; 248,608 × $1,372.34
$341,174,702

Total Direct Costs $24,384,347,302

INDIRECT COSTS

Statistical Justification Data

Special Education
Rationale: More than 22 percent of abused children have a learning disorder requiring special education. Total cost per child for learning disorders is $655 per year.

Calculations: 1,553,800 × 0.22 = 341,386; 341,386 × $655
$223,607,830

Mental Health and Health Care
Rationale: The health care cost per woman related to child abuse and neglect is $8,175,816/163,844 = $50. If the costs were similar for men, we could estimate that $50 × 185,105,441 adults in the United States cost the nation $9,255,272,050. However, the costs for men are likely to be very different and a more conservative estimate would be half of that amount.
$4,627,636,025

Juvenile Delinquency
Rationale: 26 percent of children who are abused or neglected become delinquents, compared to 17 percent of children as a whole, for a difference of 9 percent. Cost per year per child for incarceration is $62,966. Average length of incarceration in Michigan is 15 months.

Calculations: 0.09 × 1,553,800 = 139,842; 139,842 × $62,966
$8,805,291,372

Lost Productivity to Society
Rationale: Abused and neglected children grow up to be disproportionately affected by unemployment and underemployment.

Lost productivity has been estimated at $656 million to $1.3 billion. Conservative estimate is used.
$656,000,000

Adult Criminality
Rationale: Violent crime in the United States costs $426 billion per year. According to the National Institute of Justice, 13 percent of all violence can be linked to earlier child maltreatment.

Calculation: $426 billion × 0.13
$55,380,000,000

Total Indirect Costs $69,692,535,227

GRAND TOTAL COST $94,076,882,529 *Annually!*

Note: A separate 2007 study, funded by the Pew Charitable Trust, estimates the annual cost of child abuse and neglect to be $103,800,000,000—a mere $10 billion variance.

Other costs should be included because at-risk kids often grow up with illiteracy, drug and alcohol issues, mental health issues, and wind-up-in-jail issues. Look at the following facts:

- Drug abuse costs society $97,000,000,000 annually (National Clearinghouse for Alcohol and Drug Information).
- Alcohol abuse costs society $148,000,000,000 annually (National Clearinghouse for Alcohol and Drug Information).
- One full year of imprisonment costs approximately $18,400 per person (National Institute on Drug Abuse), and there are just over 2,222,331 people in federal, state, and local prisons (U.S. Department of Justice), annually costing us a grand total of $40,000,000,000 for jailing people in this country.

Although we have no annual cost figures for the following, one knows there has to be a high price tag attached to the following statistics:

- There are approximately 1,700,000 teen runaways (National Center for Missing and Exploited Children).
- One in 33 children and 1 in 8 adolescents suffer from depression (National Mental Health Association).

- Approximately 1,800 youths commit suicide each year.
- Annually, approximately 3,000,000 teens acquire a sexually transmitted disease (STD) (American Social Health Association).
- Approximately 4,000,000 teen smokers will join the ranks of 45,000,000 adult smokers (Center for Disease Control).

But we do know, according to the Center for Disease Control, that 90 percent of smoking, alcoholism, inappropriate drug use, depression, and unhealthy sexual habits start in youth. In other words, these financial concerns are more than likely seeded in the world of the Shadow Child.

The total price tag is almost too large to comprehend because it is approaching, if not exceeding, $400,000,000,000 *annually*. But what is not too large for comprehension is that we have an abundance of financial data that justifies a substantial increase in prevention and intervention funding for Shadow Children. Of that, there can be little doubt. If your child is or was one of the previous statistics, you probably needed little convincing.

Section I

Shadow Children:
Type I—The School Dropout

CHAPTER 3

Youth At Risk of Dropping Out of School

FACTS we know: According to 2010 figures from the Children's Defense Fund, two of every eight school children will graduate 4 years after entering ninth grade. The U.S. Census school enrollment projections for the year 2010 are 64,233,000 children. This means that the population currently at risk of dropping out could be as many as 12,846,600 children. However, the U.S. Department of Education states that 30 percent of America's youth will not receive a high school diploma. That comes to 19,269,900 children. How we could have this almost 6,423,300 child discrepancy is covered in Chapters 6 and 7.

The financial future of high school dropouts is grim. Figures illustrating significant differences in potential monetary success, some surprising, are included below.

Why Is Dropping Out Such a Poor Choice?

One must never underestimate the social stigma of dropping out. Unless they are successful and make it big (and very few do), no adult sincerely and seriously brags about having quit school. They are ashamed. They know society looks down on the dropout. Along with this, not always but often, come the accompanying illiteracy and narrow knowledge base of the young person who drops out.

Tragic, also, is the series of events that precede the actual moment of dropping out of school. Leading up to the moment of dropping out there had to be many quality of life issues such as boredom, confusion, fear, and angst that were faced by the young person on a daily basis. All of these painful experiences are then topped off by a loss of respect for and appreciation of what the phrase a *good education* means and the feeling that school is not only a terrible place, but that academic learning is a painful experience.

These experiences are fairly personalized issues that depend on the student and their values, attitudes, and specifics of their situation. What is standard across the population, however, is the issue of loss of income and what that brings. There are many official statistics that make this issue quite clear.

The Dollar Cost of Dropping Out of School

First, let's discuss *median* annual earning by age and the highest level of school completed. These figures are based solely on year-round, full-time workers aged 18 and over who were in the civilian labor force, worked, and had earnings in 2008 (the year of the latest data available from the U.S. Bureau of the Census).

Total Education—Males and Females Combined	Median Annual Income for Life
Dropout—no diploma	$23,500
High school diploma	$30,000
Some college	$32,000
Associate's degree	$36,000
Bachelor's degree	$46,000
Master's degree or higher	$55,000

If you believe that money enables one to have better health and prosperity, including all the emotional aspects from security to self-actualization, then the picture is pretty stark for not staying in school.

There is also quite an incentive for advancing one's education. To state it quite plainly:

- A high school diploma is worth $6,500 more per year than not having a diploma.
- Some college is worth an additional $2,000 per year.
- An Associate's degree is worth an additional $4,000 per year.
- A Bachelor's degree is worth a whopping $10,000 more per year.
- A Master's degree is worth an additional $9,000 more per year.

Note: The difference in income between a person who drops out and a person with a graduate degree is almost $31,500 per year, and for each income-earning year of their life. This comes to $1,260,000 in total—a millionaire's (and a quarter) difference.

Multiply any of the above amounts by the average number of working years in any person's life. Is this a big enough reason to do whatever it takes to keep kids in school? Think about the children they will raise when they have a family and what kind of influence that differential will make in their readiness, health, and socialization skills!

There are still bigger implications in these figures. The figures you have been viewing are for males and females combined. Let us break them out for males only. Then we will do the same for females.

The following figures are based on year-round, full-time, male workers aged 18 and over who were in the civilian labor force, worked, and had earnings in 2008:

Total Education—Males Only	Median Annual Income for Life
Dropout—no diploma	$25,000
High school diploma	$32,000
Some college	$37,000
Associate's degree	$41,000
Bachelor's degree	$55,000
Master's degree or higher	$65,000

Let us look at the same chart for females:

Total Education—Females Only	Median Annual Income for Life
Dropout—no diploma	$17,000
High school diploma	$25,000
Some college	$29,000
Associate's degree	$32,500
Bachelor's degree	$42,000
Master's degree or higher	$51,000

Now let us place the two charts side by side:

Total Education	Males	Females
Dropout—no diploma	$25,000	$17,000
High school diploma	$32,000	$25,000
Some college	$37,000	$29,000
Associate's degree	$41,000	$32,500
Bachelor's degree	$55,000	$42,000
Master's degree or higher	65,000	$51,000

Remember, this is the annual average income and must be multiplied by every year of one's life to get the full impact. The disparity is so large that it makes for a depressing message.

Start looking at female students differently. What do they need from their time in school to truly take their position as economic equals in tomorrow's world?

Implications

Explaining the gender disparity in salaries per grade level achieved could spawn much speculation and discussion, but regardless of the conclusions drawn, one can draw a clear implication from the following statistic: Each and every year in the United States, approximately 821,980 babies are born to unmarried mothers who did not complete high school (Children's Defense Fund 2005). The predictably limited resources that will be available to these mothers and their children speak volumes about being at risk of many things.

CHAPTER 4

Danger in the Shadows

HAVE you visited a school during session lately? Busy, busy, busy—a lot going on in a constant buzz of activity. I certainly do not have what it takes to do what today's teachers do. Sometimes I think what has evolved slowly over the centuries into the standard operating procedure for schools today is sheer madness. We think of it as normal only because it is prevalent and we have all been through it and have been acclimated. Think about it: A surrogate parent (teacher) sequestered all day with 25–35 foster kids in hard chairs under fluorescent lights in a room with a few square feet allocated per child. Each child comes to school not empty, but with a full and diverse menu of personal, social, familial, emotional, and psychological needs ready to project onto the day (and one another). Add to this that subject matter is the last thing they want to focus on each of the 180 days they come to school.

We say to the teacher, "Be a professional, forget your personal issues, get past each kid's personal agenda, and make sure No Child Is Left Behind academically." After all the passing out of workbooks and papers, recesses and lunch, fire drills, handing in stuff, student zone-out time, sharpening pencils, announcements, and maintenance interruptions, you have maybe 3 attentive hours a day for subject matter contact time, if you are lucky. You will be held accountable, and there will be consequences if your children do not progress 9 months' worth in 8 months.

And how, in the midst of this maelstrom, are you supposed to spot Cliff Evans?

25

Cipher In The Snow[5]

It started with tragedy on a biting cold February morning. I was driving behind the Milford Corners bus as I did most snowy mornings on my way to school. It veered and stopped short at the hotel, which it had no business doing, and I was annoyed as I had to come to an unexpected stop. A boy lurched out of the bus, reeled, stumbled, and collapsed on the snow bank at the curb. The bus driver and I reached him at the same moment. His thin, hollow face was white even against the snow.

"He's dead," the driver whispered.

It didn't register for a minute; I glanced quickly at the scared young faces staring down at us from the school bus. "A doctor! Quick! I'll phone from the hotel . . ."

"No use, I tell you, he's dead." The driver looked down at the boy's still form. "He never even said he felt bad," he muttered. "Just tapped me on the shoulder and said, real quiet, 'I'm sorry. I have to get off at the hotel.' That's all. Polite and apologizing like."

At school, the giggling, shuffling morning noise quieted as news went down the halls. I passed a huddle of girls. "Who was it? Who dropped dead on the way to school?" I heard one of them half-whisper.

"Don't know his name. Some kid from Milford Corners," was the reply.

It was like that in the faculty room and the principal's office. "I'd appreciate your going out to tell the parents," the principal told me. "They haven't a phone, and anyway, somebody from the school should go there in person. I'll cover your classes."

"Why me?" I asked. "Wouldn't it be better if you did it?"

"I didn't know the boy," the principal admitted levelly. "And in last year's sophomore personalities column I noted that you were listed as his favorite teacher."

I drove through the snow and cold down the bad canyon road to the Evans's place and thought about the boy, Cliff Evans. His favorite teacher! I thought. He hasn't spoken two words to me in 2 years! I could see him in my mind's eye all right, sitting back there in the last seat in my afternoon literature class. He came in the room by himself and left by himself. "Cliff Evans," I muttered to myself, "a boy who never

---

[5]Based on a true story by Jean Mizer in 1964, adapted by Carol Lynn Pearson in 1973 as a script for an educational film by the same name, produced by Brigham Young University and distributed by Encyclopedia Britannica.

talked." I thought a minute. "A boy who never smiled. I never saw him smile once."

The big ranch kitchen was clean and warm. I blurted out my news somehow. Mrs. Evans reached blindly toward a chair. "He never said anything about bein' ailing."

His stepfather snorted. "He ain't said nothin' about anything since I moved in here."

Mrs. Evans pushed a pan to the back of the stove and began to untie her apron. "Now hold on," her husband snapped. "I got to have breakfast before I go to town. Nothin' we can do now, anyway. If Cliff hadn't been so dumb, he'd have told us he didn't feel good."

After school, I sat in the office and stared blankly at the records spread out before me. I was to read the file and write the obituary for the school paper. The almost bare sheets mocked the effort. Cliff Evans, white, never legally adopted by stepfather, five young half-brothers and sisters. These meager strands of information and the list of "D" grades were all the records had to offer.

Cliff Evans had silently come in the school door in the mornings and gone out the school door in the evenings, and that was all. He had never belonged to a club. He had never played on a team. He had never held an office. As far as I could tell, he had never done one happy, noisy kid thing. He had never been anybody at all.

How do you go about making a boy into a zero? The grade school records showed me. The first- and second-grade teachers' annotations read, "Sweet, shy child," "timid, but eager." Then the third-grade note had opened the attack. Some teacher had written in a good, firm hand, "Cliff won't talk. Uncooperative. Slow learner." The other academic sheep had followed with "dull," "slow-witted," "low I.Q." They became correct. The boy's I.Q. score in the ninth grade was listed at 83. But his I.Q. in the third grade had been 106. The score didn't go under 100 until the seventh grade. Even the shy, timid, sweet children have resilience. It takes time to break them.

I stomped to the typewriter and wrote a savage report pointing out what education had done to Cliff Evans. I slapped a copy on the principal's desk and another in the sad, dog-eared file. I banged the typewriter and slammed the file and crashed the door shut, but I didn't feel much better. A little boy kept walking after me, a little boy with a peaked, pale face; a skinny body in faded jeans; and big eyes that had looked and searched for a long time and then had become veiled.

I could guess how many times he had been chosen last to play sides in a game, how many whispered child conversations had excluded him, how many times he hadn't been asked. I could see and hear the faces that said over and over, "You're nothing, Cliff Evans."

A child is a believing creature. Cliff undoubtedly believed them. Suddenly, it seemed clear to me: When finally there was nothing left at all for Cliff Evans, he collapsed on a snow bank and went away. The doctor might list "heart failure" as the cause of death, but that wouldn't change my mind.

We couldn't find 10 students in the school who had known Cliff well enough to attend the funeral as his friends. So the student body officers and a committee from the junior class went as a group to the church, being politely sad. I attended the services with them and sat through it with a lump of cold lead in my chest and a big resolve growing through me.

I've never forgotten Cliff Evans or that resolve. He has been my challenge year after year, class after class. I look for veiled eyes or bodies scrounged into a seat in an alien world. "Look, kids," I say silently. "I may not do anything else for you this year, but not one of you is going to come out of here as a nobody. I'll work or fight to the bitter end doing battle with society and the school board, but I won't have one of you coming out of there thinking himself a zero."

Most of the time—not always, but most of the time—I've succeeded.

And then there was Don Cheney, a personal experience I will share with you.

Don Cheney (1941–1955)

I attended junior high school in a small Ohio town. In the eighth grade, one frosty Monday November morning, I came to school, and students in homeroom were already buzzing about Don Cheney. Seems his parents found him hanging in the family barn on Saturday morning, with a carefully made baling-twine noose nailed into a rafter around his neck and a kicked-over stepladder underneath him.

"What's going on?" I said to my buddy Larry who sat behind me in homeroom.

"Don Cheney hung himself!" Larry exclaimed. "Didn't leave a note or nothin'!"

I can still remember my thoughts at the time. I ruminated to myself, *Don Cheney. Don Cheney? Now who the heck was Don Cheney?*

This is most remarkable since I had been in this school for 3 years with Don Cheney. There were only about 90 boys in the whole eighth grade, and he was in my cohort group homeroom!

"Which one was Don Cheney?" I asked Larry, looking around to see if I could discern who was missing. I couldn't.

"He was that white-headed kid—sat over there by the blackboard," Larry pointed to an empty chair along the side wall.

I still couldn't quite place him.

Larry continued, "He was that quiet kid, the one that always ran by himself in PE." Bingo! Then I remembered him. When we ran laps in Frysinger's gym class we always ran with a buddy to chat with—sometimes in little cliques of three or four. But Cheney always ran by himself in the back of the pack, never speaking to anyone.

I then remembered that I didn't even know the sound of his voice—and that's saying something for the typical male mid-kid who usually can't shut up for more than a nanosecond!

But Don Cheney never said anything to anyone. He sat by himself in the cafeteria. All of our classes were together, and he never raised his hand in class to contribute, nor did he ever raise it to ask for help. He just sat along the side of the room and kept to himself.

Even in death, he kept it all quiet. No one ever knew why on a bitterly cold Saturday morning, Don set his alarm early even for a farm kid, and all alone, this 14-year-old boy, wearing only a T-shirt, jeans, and tennis shoes, went out to the barn and hanged himself.

It haunts me to this day—almost 50 years later—as if it were yesterday.

Don Cheney will always be one of the posters in my head for Shadow Children.

Shadow Children, if noticed, are often classified by school systems as being *at risk*. They are not special education students and often do not have any of the alphabetic designations, such as LD, ED, BD, ADD, or ADHD. The original label of *at risk* derived from students being seen as at risk of dropping out of school. Schools have rarely addressed the issue of students dropping out who were not identified as at risk prior to dropping out. These students had obviously been at risk, but no one noticed. The criteria were obviously incorrect. Why wouldn't a school system, the center of *learning* in a community, be the first to learn from its own glaring miscalculation?

Many states and agencies have played with various definitions of the term *at risk*. Some districts use the term easily, others awkwardly, and some are in denial and have stated for the record that they do not have any at-risk students. One case I can think of is a high school with over 2,000 students that claimed it had no students at risk. This was despite the fact that they graduated 200 fewer seniors than their entering freshmen count 4 years earlier. One might politely call this practice "fudging." As some school districts try to deny the existence of the Shadow Children or at least narrow the definition, others are fighting to bring the accurate count of at-risk youth into the light and even expand the definition.

The point of view of this book is that we need to find a way to clearly answer two questions:

1. How can you begin to know what you did not know? In other words, how can we begin to spot these students at risk of not succeeding in school and/or not succeeding in life *prior* to them becoming a statistic?
2. What kind of prevention/intervention practices/programs should be instituted?

Let us begin to answer the first question by clearly defining what we mean by *at risk* and what the lead-ups are to becoming at risk. Later we will look at the means by which we can educationally intervene, and deliberately and consistently save these children thereby offering them a chance at a life commensurate with the American Dream.

CHAPTER 5

Expand the Definition of At Risk?
Are You Crazy?

A S a first-year high school biology teacher I was eager to do well. As someone who avidly prepares for everything, I was consuming data in great haste during the August teacher week prior to the students' return to school, including poring over each student's "cume" folder. A yellow jacket-style folder that was the only means of tracking a student in the school system prior to the use of computers, a student's cumulative folder held their major achievement scores, their I.Q. scores, final grades in grade levels and/or courses completed. Teachers were also required to include their comments about each student at the end of the year. This was to help the next teacher get an idea of the students they were inheriting. It was a system fraught with fault and a setup for potential disaster.

Most teachers, eager to get out of school in June after the students left for the summer, put down a hurried sentence in the required space—sometimes only a phrase. Base covered. You had to write something—you wrote what quickly came to mind. *Next Folder!* What, you're expecting nobility?

I remember sitting in my biology classroom at one of the student lab tables with the stack of yellow folders, one for each of the students in my six classes of sophomore biology. Being new to the town (and teaching), I wanted to know all I could about the students I were to meet.

I had never been impressed by letter grades. With age, I would become even more unimpressed with both letter grades and the "grades" that differentiated groups by age from kindergarten through the senior year: Grades K–12.

Then, as a certified teacher, I was much more fascinated with the teacher comments that had followed these students for 10 years. I quickly went through the pile, reading what last year's teachers had written to help me "get to know" my students in advance of their coming to class.

I remember reading about Barry Boedecker, a Future Farmers of America (FFA) member and member of the vocational-education track, as opposed to the general, business, or college preparatory track. Barry's freshman English teacher had written that Barry was trouble. *Hmmm.* This was important to know. Everyone knew the FFA boys were a wild bunch and, lucky me, Barry Boedecker was in my biology class. I knew I had better keep an eye on *him.*

The dark blue jacket with the gold embroidery worn by FFA members was the traditional garb of the farm boys at Hendersonville High and easy to spot. They wore them everywhere, every day. They were a proud Wild Bunch of Ohio farm boys. Barry was easy to spot as he had his name embroidered above the left-breast pocket of his jacket, plus he was the only FFA student in my class.

I learned firsthand that the previous teacher had been correct. Barry was a handful. I nailed him with reprimands at least five times in the first week: *Stop talking, Barry. Give me that note, Barry. Be quiet, Barry. Are you chewing gum, Barry? Are you chewing gum again, Barry? Stay after school tomorrow, Barry.*

Sitting in the teachers lounge on the Monday afternoon of the second week of school, I did what so many teachers used to do in the lounge—lament. As a young teacher with all these veterans sitting around me, I wanted to get in my two cents and show how much I belonged to this wonderful cadre of sport-coat professionals. I began to tell my tale. I was all but singing "Nobody Knows the Trouble I've Seen" as I added my fuel to the fire about *these students today.* I was building to my climactic moment, which centered around giving my first detention to Barry Boedecker.

"I should have seen it coming," I complained. "The signs were there, and Mr. Sandlin reported last year that Barry was a lot of trouble. Now I have to stay after school with him in detention!"

"Oh well," I sighed. "I can get some papers graded for that half hour."

"I am Mr. Sandlin," a voice said. I looked over the circle of cigarette smokers (most of us were) at a bespectacled, friendly face.

"Hi," I said enthusiastically, extending my hand. I was glad to meet a friendly colleague and someone who had shared with me the tribulations caused by this terrible student. Someone who would nod and agree that, indeed, Barry Boedecker was the devil incarnate and we both had one shoulder to share the professional load of responsibility for Barry's rehabilitation, if it was even possible. "I appreciate the heads up on Barry, Mr. Sandlin. He certainly is a handful. I had to give him a detention after about five infractions in one week."

Mr. Sandlin was frowning.

"I don't know what you are talking about," he said.

The circle grew silent.

"Barry Boedecker," I repeated.

"Yes, I heard that. But did you say that *I* told you Barry was a bad kid?"

Something was wrong. I was starting to get red and beginning to feel that I was almost being called a liar, which I do not deal with very well to this day and certainly not in front of my peers.

I blustered, "In last year's cume folder you wrote that Barry was trouble. I read it just a week ago. It was in your handwriting!"

Strangely, his eyes were friendly again.

"Can I see you for a moment outside? These fellas don't need us disturbing their world-shaking analysis of last Friday's football game," he joked.

We went into the hall and he extended his hand once again. "I'm Fred."

"Tony," I said, extending my hand. I was still hot under the collar. "Fred . . ."

"Let's go down to the office," Fred interrupted. He began walking.

We went into the front office, and Fred asked Inez, the indispensable, front-office lady who was on top of all paperwork in the Hendersonville High School Universe, for Barry's yellow folder.

"Come with me," Fred said, leading the way down the administrative hallway, where he found an empty counselor's office.

"Have a seat," he said, sitting behind the desk. I pulled up a chair. He handed me the folder. "Show me where I said that," he said kindly, with no malice or ego.

I opened the folder, knowing righteously that I was going to embarrass him for trying to embarrass me in public. I pulled out the papers, found the right one . . . scanned and placed it on the desk right in front of him, stabbing the handwritten comment victoriously with my forefinger.

He looked at it. He smiled lightly and pushed it back, turning the folder 180 degrees. "Read it again."

I read it out loud so he could hear it, ending with his written sentence: "Barry is trouble!"

"Read it again," Fred said.

I was getting very angry. I was ready to fight to the death in my righteousness. I was RIGHT. I had him!

I looked at the paper, took a deep breath and through indulgently gritted teeth, I deliberately and slowly read the paragraph aloud: "Barry is trouble—d."

I wanted to die. The redness of my face must have been close to that of a ripe tomato. "Oh my God," I remember thinking. "I can never go in that lounge again!" It was certainly an award winner among My Most Idiotic Moments.

Fred went on to explain that Barry came from an alcoholic family, and due to some family violence he had a steel plate in his head. His hair refused to grow so he shaved his head (long before it was fashionable). He also had what was called at that time "a club foot" and limped quite noticeably. In a high school with the eternal peer pressure to be cool and coming out of a violent, alcoholic home, all Barry had was the FFA. It was his life; the one place he could excel and be looked up to, and he worked hard to do both. In the classroom he overcompensated by wise-cracking and defying authority.

Today, I remember with embarrassment how naïve and unprepared I was to "lead children in learning" as their teacher. But Barry was a great professional lesson. It needed to happen, and today I am grateful that it happened so early in my career. I realize now I have probably made the same mistake, reading kids wrong, perhaps hundreds of times. But for me this incident was a tempering moment of my professional steel in learning to be very slow to judge, There is always another side to the story . . . or two or three.

Would you say Barry was "at risk"? Why? If you had to describe why you thought he was at risk, what would you say? Alcoholic parents? A family with a history of violence? A physical handicap or two? Acting out? None of these things count in most state definitions of at risk. Notice from this recounting that we have no idea of his GPA, or the number of credits he needed to graduate. In most states those are the only two questions asked. Actually, only the last one: Will he graduate on time?

I am going to defend that. For it's time. Here is how this at-risk term came to be. If you attend conferences and conventions in the genre of at-risk education, alternative education, charter schools, or drop-out prevention, you will notice that almost all attendees are working at the secondary level in education. That is the legacy created by a phrase that we have lived with for so long: "at risk of dropping out of school."

Originally, the term "at risk" meant being behind in a certain number of Carnegie units to the point where you would not be able to graduate and therefore were in danger of dropping out. The concept of the Carnegie unit was developed in 1906 as a measure of the amount of time a student studied a subject. For example, a total of 120 hours in one subject—meeting four or five times a week for 40 to 60 minutes, for 36 to 40 weeks each year—earns the student one unit of high school credit. Fourteen units were deemed to constitute the minimum amount of preparation that may be interpreted as 4 years of academic or high school preparation (Carnegie Foundation 2010).

In 1906, the concept of the Carnegie unit was quite progressive. It showed the school's concern for the student in relationship to his or her future. It also reminded the school that it had to *do something*. It had to inform the student that extra consideration needed to be made on his or her behalf if a high school diploma was needed and/or desired. It was a means by which the school acknowledged a need to intervene on a student's behalf and do something extra to help him or her graduate on time.

But that was 1906. You must admit, times have changed slightly. We no longer need farm boys and girls or factory workers to the extent that we needed them in the past. Then, farms and factories needed a swarm of worker bees that our country and the lives of its people depended on. If you dropped out of school there were jobs for you, if you had a strong back and hands. You had a good life if you had "a roof over your head and food in your belly" and it took work, often hard work, just to keep that home and the food on the table.

The Carnegie unit was irrelevant to people who just wanted to have a job in order to provide for themselves and their families. Again, "provide" was interpreted to mean you wanted for nothing that was needed to survive. There was no credit and, except for real estate, no loans to speak of. People paid in cash. There was pride in not accepting "handouts" and in sustaining one's self and family "by the sweat of your brow."

A high school diploma was nice to have if you were going to stay a manual laborer. A diploma was essential if you wished to go to college—move beyond being a "blue collar" worker and have a "more respectful" job. It was pretty cut and dry. "Good pay" was synonymous with "good life" and almost all were focused on the present moment. That thing called "the future" was down the road and not pertinent to most people in 1906.

Some feel the Carnegie unit was the first progressive step in education towards "showing concern" for a student's future. A lot has changed since 1906 yet we still have Carnegie units, except now we call them credits. The point: Times have changed yet schools have not changed commensurately with what our youth need today in order to succeed in tomorrow's world. Likewise, the definition of "at risk" being based on credits has changed in most states, but the *reason* for it has not changed. And this creates a problem while trying to solve one.

The National At-Risk Education Network

I am the Director of the National At-Risk Education Network (NAREN). I receive no salary for the privilege of directing this wonderful organization. I tell you this because I want you to know that my motives surrounding what I am about to say are child-centered: I believe in every fiber of my being that we have the answers to make the difference needed to save many at-risk children who are facing a much higher chance of living in poverty and pain.

NAREN stands for many principles, one of which is the expansion of the definition of what the term *at risk* means. Not only are we interested in examining the substantial issue of dropout prevention, but we are examining quality of life issues as well. Equally important, we are moving away from a narrow focus on characteristics of children and broadening the view to include the school in the definition of *at risk*.

Typically, I am met with incredulity by people when I share the idea of expanding the definition of at risk. They say in effect, "If we cannot meet the needs of this population by the narrower, traditional definition, wouldn't it be insane to expand it, thereby basically creating a still larger population whose needs we cannot address?" At first glance, this certainly appears to be so, if one is taking a linear and logical view of things.

But if there is one thing we have learned, it is that most people, and certainly at-risk children, are neither linear nor logical. Educators who have not yet learned this are steeped in daily frustration with their clientele, wondering *what is wrong with these children?* Nothing. Nothing is wrong with them except that they just don't measure up to erroneously drawn expectations—expectations that are still based on the old scope and sequence way of thinking about curriculum and the people the curriculum is *supposed* to fit. Our means of measuring this is now over 100 years old. The Carnegie unit or "Credit Deficiency" models are officially antiques.

This discrepancy between expectations and reality is even more extreme when dealing with Shadow Children. Most at-risk children are whole-to-part learners. Schools are set up in a part-to-whole assembly line fashion, which again assumes a linear and logical philosophy. Our current definitions and modalities of instruction with at-risk kids are yesterday, so yesterday that we have further decreased the chance for at-risk children to succeed, ensuring that Shadow Children will stay in the shadows.

Some wonder if we are subconsciously trying to drive at-risk kids out of schools entirely. (Technically labeled "push outs.") If this is true we need to wake up, because even if we drove them out, where would they go? They would be in our communities, but now as undereducated, alienated adults raising yet another generation of school-haters. It is essential to look at our definitions, values, and approaches to reaching the at risk so we can modernize our efforts and increase the success rate for these children.

Let us look more closely at the Shadow Children issue from this perspective of definitions. Definitions can be thought of as assessments in another form. They suggest a diagnosis of the problem and a listing of telltale symptoms. Of course, the academic and clinical rationale for clearly defining is to suggest more precise avenues of remediation.

Therefore, to differentiate the word *definition*:

- a *bad* definition = an ineffective highway of remediation
- a *good* definition = an effective highway of remediation

Old Definitions

Listed below are some of the usual and customary definitions of *at risk*.

At risk as defined by the Utah Department of Workforce Services:

- Chronic absenteeism and truancy from school
- Chronic behavior problems
- Chronic underachievement in school
- Family illiteracy
- Physical/sexual/psychological abuse

- Cultural differences
- Ethnic or racial differences
- Social/developmental immaturity
- Substance abuse
- Limited English proficiency
- Lacks occupational goals/skills
- Chronic health problems

At risk as defined by The Youth and Family Services Division of Harris County, Texas:

> In the eyes of area service providers, of the one million children (infants to 18 years) who live in Harris County at least one third are at-risk simply because they live in poverty. Risk factors range from drug use and failure in school to gang violence, abuse, learning disabilities, limited language skills and neglect.

At risk as defined by the Wisconsin Department of Public Instruction:

> At-Risk means pupils in grades 5 to 12 who are at risk of not graduating from high school because they failed the high school graduation test, are dropouts, or are two or more of the following:
>
> 1. One or more years behind their age group in the number of high school credits attained.
> 2. Two or more years behind their age group in basic skill levels.
> 3. Habitual truants.
> 4. Parents.
> 5. Adjudicated delinquents.
> 6. Eighth-grade pupils whose score in each subject area on the eighth-grade examination was below basic level, or who failed to be promoted to the ninth grade.

These three references are not uncommon. They reflect an ingrained and dangerous bias. No child ever asked to be placed at risk or aimed for it deliberately, yet these definitions treat children almost as if they chose these traits. In order to reverse this old-fashioned and detrimental defining, we must stop looking at kids' characteristics as a definition of at risk and look at the partner in the dance of at-riskness, *the school*. Some will want to shy away from this angle of vision because, at first glance, it appears that once again the poor school looks at fault, and as everyone knows, "We are doing the best we can with the little money we have."

New Definitions, New Ways

However, if we accept the NAREN definition of at risk, we effectively mode the school because this definition shows us the potential areas of impact where the school *can* do something. I am going to ask you, the reader, to *feel*—as well as see—the difference in this mode of defining *at risk*.

> *At-risk student* means: Students may be at-risk when they experience a significant mismatch between their circumstances and needs, and the capacity or availability of appropriate educational opportunities which accommodate and respond to those students circumstances and needs in a manner that supports and enables their maximum social, emotional, and intellectual growth and development.—National At-Risk Education Network

The NAREN definition allows and encourages the school to assess all children under their care to ascertain if indeed they are at risk, and then to design a compensatory program (which may or may not include an academic emphasis).

The strong implication of this definition is that, as long as you have at-risk students, the school is part of the problem, as well as the solution.

The outmoded definition of *at risk* reminds me of my work in the South during school integration issues in the late 1960's when some thought it was enough to have *equal opportunity* for children being bussed to achieve racially mixed schools. It wasn't. It helped, but it wasn't nearly enough. The children might have those new books and better teachers in the new school, but the children were *not ready* for those books, and the teachers were *not ready* for the students in many ways.

It was not until the federal government added the phrase of *attainment* that the school began to do more than just slap the new book in front of African American children and say, "There! Now you have the new book . . . read it!" Once the complete formula for compensatory education was stated as *equal opportunity of attainment* the school had to own up to the fact that they must make a genuine effort to reach the students where they are—not demand that they stretch to a level they do not have the skills to reach. At-risk kids often need the same prescription for school success: an *equal opportunity of attainment*.

To succeed, at-risk students must have an equal opportunity of attainment.

Larger Definitions

Not only do we need more depth in the definition of *at risk,* but also more breadth. NAREN accepts dropout behavior(s) as a legitimate *half* of the definition and expands it laterally by adding *being at risk of not succeeding in life due to being raised in unfavorable circumstances.* This begs the professional educator to look at the symptomologies of students coming from dysfunctional situations and understand and have compassion for them, and not punish, shame, or deny them our help because they are sporting survivor symptoms in a frequently unpleasant package. Imagine a medical doctor refusing treatment because you have a bad attitude with regard to your cancer symptoms!

We will look at this second half of the expanded definition of Shadow Children in Section II.

Conclusion

We must stretch to a new level of professionalism. We must look at different practices with paradigm-shifted viewpoints and new, contemporary definitions for at-risk education—practices and definitions that are research-based and needs-based just for at-risk students, standards and definitions that value students who never asked to be placed at risk and who look to us for coaching out of their dilemma, not punishment for finding themselves in a dilemma equipped with few, if any, skills to find their own way.

> To ask at-risk kids to be better than their parents is asking them to be heroes. Very few of us are heroes.—Jerry Conrath

The NAREN contention is that if we expand and deepen the definition and officially meet some of the nonacademic needs of Shadow Children, we may very well find the population defined by the old definitions dropping in numbers rather than the students themselves dropping out.

Almost all of us move away from that which seems adverse, unpleasant, rejecting, meaningless, and useless. One does not need research to back this up. If you have been an at-risk student you know what I mean by this. If you have never been an at-risk student—someone who has been in trouble and hurting yet on the outside looking in at the one thing that could save you, but doesn't get you at all—well, I wonder how you could. Talk to your at-risk students—if they are still in school. They will tell you firsthand.

CHAPTER 6

Counting the Shadow Children—Part I

The Dropout Scenario

THE question from the media often is, "Is the at-risk student population increasing, or staying the same, or decreasing?" It happens to also be an important question because extra funding, services, personnel, and those things that will offer equal opportunity of attainment to the at-risk population are often based on count. To have count, you must have clarity of definition. To have accurate, meaningful count, you must not only have specificity of definition, but also integrity on the part of the "counters."

Often, a complicated question is disguised as a simple one. This is one of those. If one wanted a sound-bite answer to this question, as most media people do, it would be meaningless. This may be why many educational issues discussed in the media *are* sometimes meaningless, trivialized, incoherent, and misleading.

Let me emphasize that whether the at-risk population is increasing or decreasing is a most serious question. It is a critical question because counts determine funding and programming, and more often than not, outcomes depend on proper funding and programming. Sometimes counts are about where a new highway should be routed or where a new burger place will be located. Counts mean something to the people involved, but not much to the rest of us. Highways are everywhere. Hamburgers are too. But dealing with funding and programming for at-risk children is going to be a matter of life or death to many of those children. It is as serious as a suicide or a life of poverty.

Someone meddling with the count of a bank cash drawer goes to jail—over a paper substance called dollars. Someone meddling with the count of Shadow Children gets—nothing. Nothing happens as a result. Nothing, except that kids who desperately need help and look to the authorities in education to support and defend them are denied that help and continue their downward spiral into merely statistical significance.

Count *is* important. Let's look closely at the issue. It is complex, but understandable. In order to meaningfully answer the question of whether the number of at-risk students is increasing or decreasing in the United States, one has to carefully define parameters.

The concept of the *at-risk student* count is quite amorphous, and this has helped it become a "chameleon" statistic in educational political arenas. The figures that hit the media have often been filtered and spun to place the agency releasing the figures in the best possible light. National political parties, during their administrations, will focus only on the statistics that work for them. What makes their party look good and what makes the other party or opponent look bad? Many people expect this statistical coloring among politicians, but shamefully, school administrators use these tactics as well.

Using the confusion and cloudiness created by diverse and poorly constituted definitions, school administrators who will be penalized for having large populations of at-risk kids are able to find ways to underreport those figures. State departments of education know this and up to now have mostly shrugged about it, often enabling it by both failing to establish a clear definition as to specifically what *at risk* means and by not imposing any penalties whatsoever on local districts that make false reports.

If you do not confront, you enable.

Why would a state department of education enable something as serious as misidentifying a population that is in such desperate need of assistance? Let us answer that by asking two questions:

1. How does it reflect upon a state department of education when its state's at-risk figures are higher than neighboring states?
2. What is the economic fallout for a state when its Shadow Children statistics impact the possibility of new industry locating within its borders?

The bottom line here is, obviously, the dollar and not the needs of kids. "Follow the money" is the appropriate rejoinder if you want answers regarding why we have not done a better job of solving our at-risk students' needs and why convenient confusion is allowed (or encouraged) to remain. Of course, the end result is a conspiracy, whether consciously or unconsciously formed, to push Shadow Children further into the shadows.

So, with all that being said, several angles of view need to be shared in order to answer the dropout increase/decrease question. The actual count will primarily be determined by definition and second, by effective data gathering. Honesty in reporting will be the third factor.

First, some people/agencies define at risk only as *at risk* of dropping out of school, but even this very narrow definition does not provide as much comfort as one might think. There are actually four (4) ways of defining at risk in terms of achieving a clear head-count.

1. *Event Dropout Rate:* the percentage of students who drop out of school in a given year

2. *Status Dropout Rate:* the percentage of young people (usually 16–24 years old) who are not currently enrolled in school and who do not have a diploma or GED

3. *High School Completion Rate:* the complement of the status dropout rate (one minus the status dropout rate) but based on 18–24 year olds, not 16–18 year olds

4. *Promoting Power:* the ratio of the number of students in a certain grade to the number that graduate when expected to graduate

Statistics are often warped by including GED recipients as graduates, and research shows clearly that a GED *is not* the equivalent of a high school diploma by any stretch in terms of social acceptance or, perhaps more importantly, economic gain for the recipient. Some research shows that the very existence of the GED increases dropout figures [Greene 2002, 23].

One does not expect the general public to know of all these definitions, although the impact of the differences is tremendous. A NAREN survey of over 600 teachers has found that *not a single one* knew these definitional categories existed, much less the impact created by varying the selection of a particular definition. That is reprehensible professional naiveté. Why? Because it becomes part of the unconscious conspiracy against children who need support. Unfortunately, ignorance can kill as well as a cold-hearted, deliberate murderer.

This appears to be enough confusion and chaos without even looking at the much larger definition of *at-risk youth* espoused by the National

At-Risk Education Network and laid out in the previous chapter. But going by the figures we do currently have and generously assuming that the figures reported by schools are even close to accurate, we at least have the first answer to the increase/decrease question.

Statistically Significant Indicator #1

While dropout rates for non-Hispanic whites and blacks have declined substantially (from 12 to 7 and 21 to 13 percent, respectively) between 1972 and 2000, there was no statistically significant decline among Hispanics. Twenty-eight percent of Hispanic young adults drop out before completing school. This is a tragic figure.

The final sound-bite answer here within this set of dropout count parameters would be: Things are better for whites and blacks; no change for Hispanics.

[By the way, if you're wondering which of the four definitions of dropouts this sound-bite answer is based on, it's: *The Status Dropout Rate.*]

So, to refresh your memory: Students may be at risk when they experience a significant mismatch between their circumstances and needs, and the capacity or availability of appropriate educational opportunities that accommodate and respond to them in a manner that supports and enables their maximum social, emotional, and intellectual growth and development. Again, this involves the school inside the definition, rather than outside the definition. If the Shadow Child has these *other* statistics against him or her (poverty, Alcohol and Other Drug Addiction (AODA), teen pregnancy, emotional issues, etc.) and the school cannot accommodate those symptomatic behaviors, then the school falls down and literally becomes part of the problem. With this in mind, the answer to the increase/decrease question is: The number of Shadow Children is *increasing*.

Statistically Significant Indicator #2

Following a substantial increase in participation between 1996 and 1999, the proportion of pre-kindergarten 3- to 5-year-olds attending center-based early childhood care and education programs dropped from 60 percent to 56 percent in 2001.

Why is this a problem? In 1990, the National Education Goals Panel established its first National Education Goal: "By the year 2000, all children in America will start school ready to learn." To reach this goal, the Goals Panel created three objectives for families and communities, the first of which stated that "all children will have access to high-quality and developmentally appropriate preschool programs that help prepare children for school." The Goals Panel also designated preschool participation, particularly by children living in poverty, as an indicator of progress toward this goal.

We are clearly failing here. The noble goal of the National Education Goals Panel has not been met in 2011, much less by 2000, and the eventual payoff will be disastrous because there will be a ballooning statistical cluster of children beginning school with low readiness skills—entering schools already having difficulty dealing with special needs in children. Based on statistically significant indicator #2, the answer would be: The number of Shadow Children is *increasing*.

It is clearly a pay-me-now or pay-me-later scenario, but the delayed payment will be much costlier. Meanwhile children are suffering and officials underreporting or fudging figures are taking liberal license with those lives. Each time this inaccurate reporting occurs, inefficiency and/or incompetence is covered up at the expense of accurate data that is critical to effective planning, funding, and programming for children who desperately need it. If we define crime as harming the innocent, then how could the practice of deliberately misreporting be interpreted as anything other than a criminal offense?

Section II

Shadow Children:
Type II—Unhealthy Beginnings

CHAPTER 7

Counting the Shadow Children—Part II

At Risk of Not Succeeding in Life

THERE are a variety of figures showing that if you drop out of school, it has a lifelong economic impact. This is no small matter; money is important. Money is a means to many ends: better nutrition, better health care, better housing, better education, better and safer neighborhoods, better clothing, and more. All bear on the freedom to choose a longer and healthier life. No money, few choices. More money, more choices. More education/more money does not mean a person *will* choose those things that promote a longer healthier life, but they will at least have the *opportunity* to choose those things. Education is about opportunity, more doors of opportunity to open as opposed to having just one or, perhaps, no door of opportunity.

Understand, what will be said in this chapter will probably not impress kids. That is not its purpose. Its purpose is to impress *you*. You are the one who will work harder to keep kids in school and make it more meaningful while there. You must see the long road for them. This is why we are called adults—we think abstractly and are able to foresee things that are not presently apparent. Example: If I do not save *this* money I won't have *that* service when I need it. We are the keeper of the children. We are their future eyes until they develop their own. You know it is the right thing to do *for them*. We have to be tough and intellectual for them—again—until they can be that for themselves.

Dropping out of school is not a choice we should allow.

We no longer allow children to choose to drink or smoke. Why? Because drinking and/or smoking has life-damaging consequences that children cannot foresee. So we make that decision for them by passing a statute that says No. Adults get the freedom to self-destruct if they want to, supposedly because they can see the consequences of their actions. Children, as a rule, cannot see the consequences of their actions much past the ends of their noses, so we assume *in loco parentis* powers and make laws to protect children from themselves. Dropping out of education is proven, beyond a shadow of a doubt, to have life-damaging consequences. We should never allow children to drop out of school. The data and stories to support this prohibition are abundant.

The second part of the new definition of at-risk children is that they are at risk of not succeeding in life. Why is this expansion to *at risk of dropping out* proposed?

Several years ago, a national speaker at a conference ended his lecture to a group of educators of at-risk students with this statement: "Doctors know why they are in business. Ministers know why they are in business. Dentists know why they are in business. Why is it that in our profession educators are so confused about what business we are in? Isn't that a shame?" I looked around at the other educators in my immediate area with a raised eyebrow. Seemed to me we *did* know what business we were in. But just in case the speaker was right for some educators, let us set the record straight as to what our business is: *We are in the SUCCESS business!*

Doctors promote people's physical health. Dentists promote people's oral health. Ministers promote people's spiritual health. And we educators? We promote people's ability to succeed in life. Isn't this clear to us? I hope so. But maybe it isn't. Maybe we want to stay confused so we can't feel the sting of the obvious message that, if we are in the success business and the kids (our clientele) are failing, we are obviously failing.

Q: What is your business?
A: I sell cars. I am a car salesman.

Q: How many buyers do you have?
A: Well, I don't have any buyers.

Q: Well then, how can you be a salesman?
A: Gosh, now that you put it that way, I guess I am not a salesman yet.

If we educators are in the success business, then we better start defining ourselves by that standard, don't you think? If a chain is as strong as its weakest link, isn't the following also true? *A school is as good as its worst students.* This should be our standard. It sets the bar.

We make no prisoners!

It is a high one, but with each child we save because we raised our own standards to zero tolerance for dropouts, the better that high standard looks. If we are in the success business and even some of our students spend years in our programs and *still* do not succeed, what does that say about us?

If Jim makes 100 contacts with potential buyers and sells no cars, he is no salesman. If Sally makes 100 contacts with potential buyers and sells 100 cars, she is substantially better than Jim.

Question: What does Jim with zero sales say when he hears about Sally's 100 sales?

1. Wow, Sally is getting better clients than I do. It has nothing to do with me.
2. Clients are not what they used to be.
3. This place sucks. I'm glad vacation is coming because I need it.
4. I have a lot to learn obviously. Maybe Sally will show me how she reaches her clients so effectively.

What should we say to ourselves as professionals when we discover that some of our students are not succeeding in life after spending 12 of their most formative years with us for the express purpose of success preparation?

A New Starfish Story

A fellow is walking down the beach on his lunch hour. He and his business partner are in their suits—their shoes and socks neatly sitting on the beach, their pants cuffs rolled up, suit coats slung over their shoulders—getting some fresh ocean air and a bit of exercise and pondering a problem that needs to be addressed back at the office. It is a casual stroll; the sun is finally shining after a large storm that passed earlier in the morning. As they walk, one of the men keeps bending over to pick up the starfish that have washed ashore and throw them back into the ocean.

The shorter of the two men is very involved with the business problem, barely noticing they are on the beach. After the taller fellow has bent over and picked up about 20 starfish, the shorter fellow is the one with the red face, frustrated with his partner's divided attention. Finally he blurts out, "Bob, what are you doing?"

"Bill, I think it is obvious. I am throwing starfish back into the ocean before they shrivel up and die."

Bill says, still frustrated, "I know that, but why bother? There are hundreds of them. What does it matter?"

Bob turns to Bill and, wiggling the current starfish under Bob's turned-up nose before he throws it back into the ocean, says, "It certainly matters to this one."

Bill says, "Oh, please . . ."

And Bob looks Bill squarely in the eye and says, "And it matters to *me*."

As a parent, an educator, a citizen, or anyone who is an adult: We save one kid at a time because it matters to us. That is what counts. We see down the road, we see disaster coming, and it matters that children are playing hopscotch in the middle of a highway. It matters to us. That is all the justification you need to learn the following.

Youth At Risk from a Bad Start

Talk to any experienced elementary teacher, and he or she will tell you they can spot at-risk children easily in the K–3 grades. Almost all of these children come from homes of poverty, neglect, and/or abuse. This is usually not a revelation to anyone.

Facts we know[6]:

- Over 1,000,000 of the 3,092,000 reports of child abuse or neglect made to Child Protective Service agencies are verified in the United States each year. One can only guess how many go unreported or *are* true but lack verification. Without a doubt, the actual numbers of abused and neglected children are much higher. ChildHelp, a national organization that is as on top of these numbers as well as anyone can be, states that the actual number of children being abused is at least three times this much (2010). Based on the tables of Classification System of Child Abuse and Neglect (CSCAN) in Appendix I, my guess is that it is at least 10 times—even 100. If you accept the CSCAN, then every child is

[6]*Source:* Children's Defense Fund 2009; Children's Defense Fund 2010b.

abused probably every day. At some point statistics become meaningless and we develop zero tolerance and do all we can to stop all incidents. The same can be said for a lot of statistics. These are all verifiable, documented, and visible to the naked eye.

- 13,500,000 children live in poverty—or about one in five (18.9 percent).
- 512,000 babies are born to teen mothers each year.
- 2,100,000 children are arrested each year.
- An estimated 1,600,000 children in the United States have an imprisoned father, and 200,000 have an imprisoned mother. Most children with incarcerated parents live in poverty before, during, and after their parents' incarceration. (See the Prisons, Parents, and Pupils section below.)
- 26 percent of 12th graders, 22 percent of 10th graders, and 12 percent of 8th graders have used illicit drugs in the previous 30 days.
- 31 percent of 12th graders, 26 percent of 10th graders, and 15 percent of 8th grade students reported having five or more alcoholic beverages in a row in the previous 2-week period.
- Every 5 hours in the United States another youth commits suicide. Besides the tragic loss of another young individual, the act of suicide itself devastatingly impacts the dozens of friends and relatives left behind.

All of the children included in the above statistics (and more categories not listed) come to school carrying their burdens and issues with them. It is safe to assume that many of the children represented in the above figures are, indeed, at risk of having decreased horizons of success. By default, our schools have become the focus of efforts to address serious issues of Shadow Children. Schools readily admit they are both inadequately informed and inadequately prepared for this immense task, but this has not stopped many of them from making the noble effort *because it matters to them.*

A special note on children with imprisoned parent(s).

Prisons, Parents, and Pupils

In 2008, corrections was the fastest expanding major segment of state budgets, and over the past two decades its growth as a share of state expenditures has been second only to Medicaid. State corrections costs now top $50 billion annually and consume 1 in every 15 discretionary dollars. The remarkable rise in corrections spending wasn't fate or even the natural consequence of spikes in crime. It was the result of state policy choices that sent more people to prison and kept them there longer. The sentencing and release laws passed in the 1980s and 1990s put so many more people behind bars that last year the incarcerated population reached 2.3 million and, for the first time, 1 in 100 adults was in prison or jail (Pew 2009).

The escalation of the prison population has been astonishing, but it hasn't been the largest area of growth in the criminal justice system. That would be probation and parole—the sentenced offenders who are not behind bars. With far less notice, the number of people on probation or parole has skyrocketed to more than 5 million, up from 1.6 million just 25 years ago. This means that 1 in 45 adults in the United States is now under criminal justice supervision in the community. This, combined with those in prison and jail, means a stunning 1 in every 31 adults, or 3.2 percent, is under some form of correctional control. The rates are drastically elevated for men (1 in 18) and blacks (1 in 11) and are even higher in some high crime, inner city neighborhoods (Pew 2009).

Why, you might ask, are there so many "ex-cons" walking our streets, living in our neighborhoods, and sending kids to our schools?

Federal prison facilities are operating at 37 percent above rated capacity, system wide, as of January 11, 2007. The federal inmate population has increased dramatically over the past 25 years, up nearly 700 percent, from approximately 25,000 inmates and 41 institutions in 1980 to 193,616 inmates and 114 institutions as of January 11, 2007 (U.S. Department of Justice 2008). Note, that is just *federal* inmates. There are another 2.1 million in state and local lockups.

And, on average, for each adult in prison there is one child on the outside. As of 2008, there are 2.3 million incarcerated adults and approximately 2 million children left behind (Pew 2009). Dr. Cindy Poehlman from the School of Human Ecology at University of Wisconsin-Madison (2010), finds from her research that most are black. By age 14, *about half of black children with a parent who dropped out of school also have a parent in prison.*

Based on her interviews with children and substitute caregivers in more than five Midwestern cities, Dr. Poehlman finds a possible amelioration with a mentoring program. Her action research showed a direct correlation between contacts with mentors and fewer behavioral problems in school within just a 6-month period. (For guidelines on how to set up a mentoring program at your school, read about the Secret Angel Club in a later chapter.)

The Educational War We Are In

The Angel-Warrior At-Risk Educator Code

We literally are in a war to save many of our children. Our enemies are many. Our first goal is to gain clarity about our goals. This clarity includes knowing our enemies, the first of which is *ignorance.*

How Do We Arm Ourselves?

1. We must develop an unbridled, unstoppable, impassioned, intelligent, and persistent effort to lower these figures in any way we can, child by child.
2. We must develop an internal locus of control for ourselves and seek out other colleagues and interested citizens who are determined to proactively make a difference.
3. We must learn about Shadow Children, their academic, psychological and social issues, and their individual learning needs and styles.
4. We must become serious about the education of children as a preventative matter, not only on a minute-by-minute basis, but comprehensively pre-K–12 and beyond.
5. We must be the champions to children that they need in order to develop healthfully. We need to get close to them rather than turn away; talk to them about important things in their lives rather than ignore them; and let them know we care rather than act like we wish they would disappear.
6. In other words, we need to embrace these children and clearly send the message that we want them, need them, and, above all, love them.

This book has been written to help arm educational stakeholders with the knowledge necessary to provide the avenues of liberation so desperately needed by our youth.

It is a glorious war we are in. It is all about the things of which great fiction are often made, except *this* war is very real. It is about rescuing the helpless, rooting out decay, and replacing it with marvelous life enhancements. It often comes down to good triumphing over some form of evil. It is about saving lives. What could be more exciting or worthwhile than that? How many professionals get the chance to dedicate themselves to such a worthy cause?

Unfortunately, it is often a thankless job, with long and unbroken stretches of solitary work. As service workers we must often sustain ourselves, but we must also make the effort and time to network with our colleagues not only to share information that might expedite our work, but also to inspire one another with our hope, strength, and experience.

Above all, we must be courageous, intelligent, and persistent Angel-Warrior Educators.

CHAPTER 8

Understanding the Effects of
Abuse and Neglect

FREEDOM of choice is power. Shadow Children, many of whom are survivors of dysfunctional families, are often raised in ignorance and they become shackled by that ignorance—ignorance about emotions, relationships with people and self, limits and boundaries, and other essential tools and skills necessary for a thriving life. This ignorance—again, one of our main enemies in this battle—leaves each survivor with limited choices and, therefore, limited power. Their universe has been artificially restricted by unenlightened caregivers who, perhaps unintentionally, have constricted to a mere slice what life has to offer these Shadow Children, and what they will, without intervention, have to offer back to the world.

This book is not about building yet another case as to what trouble our youth are in, or laying blame here and there. I think most people know by now that it is the fault of society/parents/the media/the schools/God/poor nutrition and allergies. Enough grousing, whimpering, carping, and other animal sounds have been expressed, and still the problem exists in record numbers.

Q: Why have we not been able to make a substantial dent in these horrifying statistics?
A: We have failed to understand the psychological and societal dynamics that birth these problems again and again.

Q: What do we need to know?
A: We need to thoroughly understand the vulnerable attack points of these issues.

Q: Who needs this understanding?
A: Educators and educational stakeholders, especially parents—all

those desiring to be specially prepared champions of our children. Eventually, the bearers of the symptoms themselves must have understanding if they are to take charge of their symptoms, their recovery, and their lives.

Q: What forms of understanding would be most useful?

A: We need teachers fortified with the techniques, processes, practices, and programs that will and can be used to specifically benefit our youth, regardless of age level or content area. We need stakeholders sharing their time, resources, ideas, and enthusiastic support.

This section of the book is a concentrated focusing on the effects of abuse within and around the victim. The concern is not with blame but, instead, with the *dynamics* of abuse and neglect, their after effects and how, once started, these dynamics develop an identity of their own. This identity, known here as the Shadow Child Syndrome, impacts both the victim's life and the lives of those around the victim. The impact of this intra- and interpersonal virus is deadening at best and deadly at worst. It is so critical that we understand the dynamics of the long-term effects of abuse and neglect that we must temporarily suspend our concerns with fault-finding, social implications, and litigation issues. In this way, we can impartially and objectively see what lies behind the veil of this virulent syndrome.

In our world today, there appears to be more protection for perpetrating adults than for their helpless victims, especially when the abuser is a parent. It is incredible that we still find a "children-as-chattel" mentality surviving, to the detriment of our children's welfare. The goal herein is to disseminate a psychodynamic understanding of the consequences of abuse and neglect. With such understanding we can better focus our resources to more effectively champion children.

There are those who deny the need for understanding dysfunctional family survivor dynamics, usually while carefully tending their own symptoms. Some of us wonder what keeps these fellow human beings so blind to their own condition, often appearing righteous in their misery. Some call it arrogance; some call it denial. It is as if they are incapable of seeing the impact of such devastation in their own and others' lives: "Yes, I'm miserable. There may or may not be help, but I'm not going to avail myself of it." Perhaps this section can help remove the blinders of denial. There is much to gain, namely freedom and power, and little to lose, except for old pain and the fatigue of carrying around heavy and unnecessary baggage that should have been dropped long ago.

Survivors of abuse and neglect eventually manifest what is termed the Shadow Children Syndrome. There are several chapters dedicated to exploring the implications of this syndrome and how its symptoms are brought to school. Within the framework provided by this book's purposes is also a proposed nomenclature of abuse and neglect, so the reader can become familiar with the forms of abuse. It's not fun reading, but if you want to recognize trouble when you see it, you have to see it in advance. Oncologists must become familiar with cancer before they see it in a patient, if they are to be effective in bringing about a cure. Educators, likewise, may have to look at some forms of abuse to know it when they see it. More in-depth coverage and resources are found in the bibliography.

There are some unpleasant truths in this book. Fortunately, the flipside of this information is that it allows one to do something about the burdensome baggage. Internalizing the information in this book can help the individual avoid denial, the carrier of all dysfunctionality, and can facilitate effective intervention to put an end to what often becomes a vicious cycle of abuse and neglect.

CHAPTER 9

Dysfunctionality

THE word *dysfunctional* may be descriptive, but it is limiting because it sounds like broken or damaged goods. Many people automatically think the word refers to the most degenerative of families, but it applies in some ways to a majority of families. A critic of what was at one time faddishly called the Adult Child Movement sarcastically exclaimed, "Why don't you just say that anybody with less than perfect parents becomes an Adult Child?" Tongue-in-cheek or not, this is a fairly accurate statement.

Almost anyone with less than perfect parents as a child can have unfinished business as an adult, and on the way to becoming an adult. The further from perfect your parents were (in other words, the more non-cherishing moments you had as a child), the more unfinished business you can have as an adult. Recovery is not a matter of defending or blaming parents (although this may be a stage some adults need to work through) but is, rather, a matter of taking responsibility for getting on with life. Getting on with life may necessitate figuring out what is lacking in one's toolbox of life skills because of those historical deprivations and then doing some compensatory work—work that is well worth the effort if one believes that daily vitality is a desirable goal.

It is perhaps best to think of functionality on a scale from low to high. The notion that all families can be divided into just the two categories of functional and dysfunctional is dualistic and, therefore, overly simplistic and misleading. Most families have moments of high functionality as well as moments of low functionality. The higher the proportion of low-functioning moments (episodes of abuse and neglect) to high-functioning moments (episodes of affirmation and nurturance) during child-raising years, the greater the possibility of unfinished business for the individual in his or her development.

Another factor that must be considered is the level of traumatization created within the individual. This is a mysterious and extremely individualistic factor. Some children walk away from trauma unscathed. Some people walk away apparently unscathed, only to discover later that they had unconsciously repressed or consciously suppressed the effects of the trauma. When the effects of trauma are buried, they often surface later in life. We call this usually unwelcome surfacing *activation.*

Sometimes the activation is obviously related to historical abuse and neglect, but more often, it exhibits itself in a non-straightforward manner, as described in the eight characteristics of the Shadow Child Syndrome and in Chapter 13 on the implications of the syndrome for educators. Once a child gets activated, they may "act out" with behaviors that help provide some release from the pressure of emotional activation. An example of this is a child who was sexually abused becoming promiscuous whenever he or she experiences feelings of shame. The feeling of shame is activation, and the promiscuity is the acting out as a subconscious means to reduce the pressure of this powerful emotion.

Of course, some people don't walk away from trauma at all, and it is quite apparent that they have been damaged, perhaps in many ways, by what has happened to them. Psychiatric hospitals, doctors' offices, and prisons are full of these victims exhibiting unfinished business, each in their own way. As the Berlin Wall was a constant reminder of just how terrible Communism could be, so are the painful statistics of our institutions a constant monument to the cruelty against children. The righteousness exhibited by the abusers, neglectors, and their enablers will never be sufficient to camouflage the glaring statistics of our health and penal institutions, which are filled with survivors of abuse and neglect. The silenced voices of those who did not survive should be the loudest testimony of all.

Functional vs. Dysfunctional

There has always been heated debate over what a functional family is, or is not. We are going to clear that up here. One thing we can say is that a functional family is *not* dysfunctional. What is meant by this is that a functional family is not abusive or neglectful. The Classification

System of Child Abuse and Neglect (CSCAN) tables in Appendix I make clear which behaviors are abusive/neglectful.

What also obfuscates a clear-cut definition in our modern society is that who or what constitutes a family can often be quite amorphous. Academically speaking, there is no such thing as a family. There is a collection of individuals to whom we attach the name *family*. Individuals are changing each minute. One need only reflect upon oneself: we change moods, needs, thoughts, words, and behaviors constantly. How would one clearly define what a person is? We could say people vary, or the definition depends on when you take a snapshot view of an individual. One minute they are this and the next minute they are that. Multiply this across how many persons are in this collective thing labeled *family* and grasp the difficulty in clearly defining what a family is. It changes from minute to minute just as the people in it constantly change.

One must feel a bit of empathy for the Bureau of the Census as they try to compose a questionnaire so effective that everyone can put themselves into the right box when it comes to the family category. This is probably why they finally settled for the term *household*. How many people live in the apartment or house that you own or for which you pay rent? Asking the question that way gets them off the hook. And if the Bureau of the Census cannot figure out what a family is, how is the ordinary citizen to figure it out? We just assume that all families are like our family. They are not. Families are hugely different from one another, and their effects on the children are hugely different as well.

One way to think of a family is like that of an assembly line. General Motors brings their raw material, parts, tools, workers, and designs to the beginning of the assembly line, and they do not expect a Ford to pop out at the end. At the end of the assembling process, they get what they put into the assemblage all the way down the line. It is not much different with families. Submitting developing children to abuse and neglect and expecting loving, caring, healthy young adults to pop out at the end is delusional. The Ward Cleaver/Bill Cosby family is long gone. How gone is it?

1. Divorce rates in the United States are now at 50 percent (Baker 2010).
2. Unmarried women commonly bear and rear 34 percent of the nation's children (U.S. Bureau of the Census 2009).

3. If there are two parents in the home, dual-career parents are the norm (Sloan 2010).

4. Only 30 percent of families have one biological parent working at home with the other parent in a career outside the home (Weissberg et al. 2003).

What do the statistics say about the state of kids today (in addition to the alarming numbers in Chapter 1)?

1. During the course of any year, 1 of every 5 children experiences symptoms of a mental disorder (U.S. Department of Health and Human Services 1999). Less than 25 percent of these children receive appropriate services. (But they still come to school!)

2. Among 14–17 year olds, 30 percent engage in multiple high-risk behaviors in any one year, and another 35 percent are considered medium-risk, being involved with one or two problem behaviors (Dryfoos 1997).

3. 19 percent of U.S. children live in poverty. This figure represents 14,068,000 children, an increase of 700,000 over the previous year (Children's Defense Fund 2010b).

4. There are approximately 59,000,000 children in K–12 schools in the United States today. Over the last 30 years, the non-Hispanic Caucasian population has declined 16 percent, from 79 percent to 63 percent. The African American population in schools has increased 2 percent, from 14 percent to 16 percent. The Hispanic population has increased from 6 percent to 15 percent. The Asian and Pacific Islander population has expanded from 1 percent to 5 percent. The dropout rate for Hispanics is 37 percent, compared to 18 percent for African Americans and 10 percent for Caucasians (U.S. Bureau of the Census 2000).

5. Drug, alcohol, and tobacco usage is increasing in teenagers: 29 percent of teenagers reported using illegal drugs (marijuana, cocaine, heroin, hallucinogens, and others) at least once in the 2008–2009 school year, compared with 28 percent the year before. Cigarette use increased slightly to 29 percent in the 2008–2009 school year, from 28.1 percent the year before. Underage drinking is consistent: 50 percent of teens drink alcohol illegally (Pride Surveys 2009).

Many of these statistics (and those in Chapter 1) have been a result of family dysfunction. So, maybe it is time now for us to clearly see the difference between:

Functional  Dysfunctional

The format of X versus Y is useful for bringing distinctive and crystal clarity to what differentiates a functional family from a dysfunctional family.

Unfortunately, such formats can also be misleading. As mentioned before, families are dynamic and ever changing. To statically call a family functional or another family dysfunctional might make for engaging journalism but in reality, at any moment in time, one family could suddenly shift categories. Sometimes even the best (most functional) of families fall apart under pressure and do something they later regret. Or sometimes it just cannot be helped.

The story is told of Picasso's family, often represented as a most functional and, therefore, loving family, basically coming unglued during a series of horrendous earthquakes to hit Malaga, Spain, when Picasso was 3 years old. Hiding underground, his family was frantic and anxious to the point that, in front of little Pablo, Picasso's mother bore Picasso's sister Lola prematurely on a basement floor on Christmas Day. Not only did this affect Picasso and influence his painting, but his sister Lola became known affectionately as Little Earthquake to the family and friends who survived. In Picasso's famous painting *Guernica* we can see what might have happened in the mind of the 3-year-old child while he was watching the dying people and horses and listening to the children screaming for help on the long walk to the shelter (Miller 1998).

Suffice it to say that the past is truly not in the past. How much we carry with us into the future and how it affects us is determined by a mysterious equation based on factors in our vulnerability, our resiliency, and the failure of personal tools and coping skills to develop, which we need later in life.

After years of counseling work, research in the field of human psychology, and polling the best brains in the field of family systems, NAREN proposes the following eight universal category continua for judging family health. It is based on how people in the family regard and treat one another. Most families probably fall somewhere in the middle of each pairing. It is not so much how family members act once in a while as it is what the *normed* behaviors are on a fairly constant basis. It is the near-daily, consistent, and persistent messages that are actively driven into the heads of children—passively taken in and regularly absorbed subliminally—that do damage or good!

It is interesting to note that at a staff-development workshop at a Milwaukee high school, a faculty member, referring to the list of dysfunctional characteristics I had shown on a slide, suddenly exclaimed: "That's our faculty! That's us!" More scrutiny followed by other workshop members, which led to comments such as, "No wonder it's like it is around here" and "We should hang this in our lounge."

Functional	Dysfunctional
• Affirms one another	• Critical of one another
• Refuses to abuse	• Righteously abuses
• Provides quality time	• Dedicated elsewhere
• Necessities provided	• Neglects basic needs
• Health needs met	• Health needs neglected
• Problems are opportunities	• Problems weaken
• It's okay to make mistakes	• Mistakes spotlighted/shamed
• Rides easy in the saddle	• Hypervigilance as a way of life

Affirmation

We all come into the world hardwired with the need for affection, nurturing, and cherishing, that is, affirmation in all of its forms. We are not pre-programmed for rejection, abuse, or neglect. When we run up against these experiences we usually find ways to cope and survive, but many of our coping attempts, despite being earnest, are warped reactions. We keep using them anyway.

Affirmation is the most positive form of human regard. The scale goes like this:

Intolerance ➜ Tolerance ➜ Acceptance ➜ Affirmation

We are born ready for affirmation, meaning that we're ready to accept "I love you and value your uniqueness just the way you are." Intolerance is at the opposite end of affirmation, and it says to the child, "I detest you as you are; change or be in danger." Does a child know how to change in response to this? No, because the tendency of the infant human being is to just *be*.

Tolerance says, in effect, "I don't really want you around, but the law, culture, family, or spouse, says I must put up with you. Don't expect me to like the mandate or you."

Acceptance is "nice" and it surpasses intolerance or mere tolerance, but it still shows a distance in a family—polite distance, but a distance nevertheless. "You are a child, and I cannot expect you to be anything else, just yet. Someday you will grow up and not be such an acceptable bother."

Affirmation is about commemoration. It says, in effect, "Wow! Some people from India are moving in next door. Cool! How long before you think I can go over there and get to know them?"

Affirmation is unconditional approval of something or someone *exactly as they are.* Affirmation does not ask you to change but, rather, celebrates you and wishes there were more just like you. Affirmation is what infants come into the world expecting. Basically, infants expect a brass band in the delivery room, confetti, and long parades of applause and attention—and for it to never end. A family at its "most functional" should be like that: constantly affirming regardless of whether you were born with a birth defect, don't sleep through the night for a year, or aren't the hoped-for gender.

We are not talking about preferring other behaviors, not at all. Sure, I would have preferred that both of my sons would have slept straight through each night, waking only after I had brushed my teeth and had some coffee in the morning. I wish one of them had not almost scalped the cat with an enthusiastic grab, or stuck a screwdriver into an electrical outlet (and twisted it). But these things they do are not *them.* They are behaviors I work to help them change, but I affirm their *essence,* what makes them the unique contribution to the world that they are. It is my privilege to know them, to learn from them, to work with them, and to laugh with them. I did not always do this well, but they were always treasured, and maybe that is a good synonym for affirmation.

Is this asking too much of a family? Of course not. If you are not prepared to affirm children, don't have any, because if children are not affirmed, they act out, and things get very confusing from then on. Kids do not need confusion; they need clear affirmation and direction. They need surety and confidence. Parents alone have this privilege, and if they fail, the resulting symptomatic behaviors in children, of all color and variety imaginable, quite often come to school with the child, creating chaotic and obstructive situations in what is supposed to be a learning environment.

Refusal to Abuse

Functional families are not a bunch of goofy Pollyannas. They know what one another's weaknesses and fears are, but they refuse to take advantage of these vulnerabilities. They love one another too much to inflict deliberate harm. They also may be smart enough to realize that the payoff is not worth the activity; that is, it is a bad investment of behavior. I tease you about the shape of your nose, then you cry and we spend all kinds of time reassuring you that you are okay, apologizing, and trying to set things right—so why waste energy doing it in the first place when so much energy will be wasted cleaning up after it?

Dysfunctional families look for opportunities to abuse. They may actually think it is fun in some instances, or their right in others, to hurt someone small and defenseless. They often misinterpret the Bible itself to justify doing so, such as quoting, "Spare the rod and spoil the child." Interestingly, hitting children for their own good actually is not what that statement means. In the Aramaic translation, the translation written most closely to the time of Christ, the rod was the shepherd's crook, and symbolically represented giving love and protection, rather than using it to inflict pain. People who hit children are either cowards (they know they can get away with it because kids are smaller than they are) or ignorant (because there is no research at all that says it is good for children to be hit, but there is plenty that shows the damage that can be done) or they are so full of anger they cannot help themselves and therefore need therapy, or any and all combinations of these three.

In his book, *People of the Lie,* Dr. M. Scott Peck (1983), pitches a case for a new classification in the Diagnostic and Statistic Manual of Mental Disorders (DSM) for a category of evil. He is not talking about a religious issue. Peck is making a case for righteous and deliberate abuse to be seen officially as a mental malady titled *evil* so that it can be recognized and treated. In light of this category of functional familyism, Peck's argument makes perfect sense. Shouldn't we be more concerned about this as a category than, say, nervous tics or obsessive hand washing, which do have special classifications? I am not belittling the need for treatment of nervous tics or compulsive rituals, but I am stating that people deliberately and righteously inflicting harm on others in and of itself certainly should be enough justification for a category.

Quality Time

Human energy is measured in time. Being alive means being in motion, that is, *doing* something, and we measure that state of doing by time. What did you do today? Well, I spent 20 minutes folding clothes, 1 hour going to the grocery, 8 hours sleeping, 42 minutes eating, and so on. That is how we measure our energy. Raising healthy children and tending a family effectively takes a lot of time—rather large chunks of time—dedicated to maintenance, affection, fun, health, safety, and more.

If I walked up to you on the street and said, "Say, could you give me about 40 hours a week of your time?" you would say, "What? Are you crazy? I am way too busy. I can't find 3 hours a week to get in my 30-minute walking program. How am I supposed to give you 40 hours! You're nuts!"

But people have children without ever considering this major contingency. And you must find the time, because you are going to be spending at least 40 hours a week to raise that child up to adulthood—*if* you are to do a quality job. Somewhere in there you have to not just count clothes-washing and meal-fixing, but you have to build in quality time.

What is quality time? The answer depends on the ages of the individuals and cultural norms in a family, but what it does mean in terms of common characteristics is dedicated time, aware and involved connection with one another, healthy interaction, closeness and warmth. You can see why sitting and watching television in the same room would rarely fit the definition. Just eating at the same table might not qualify. Driving somewhere in the same car might not count. The point is that quality time is meaningful and nurturing to everyone involved. This takes thought and sometimes skillful planning. How many parents do that? Not enough.

Necessities Are Provided

Abraham Maslow, among others, has done a good job of telling us straight out that we need food, water, warmth, and air. When children are severely deprived of these items, it makes headlines because it is so alarming. Children going unfed for days or being kept in suffocating closets, cages, or basements is shocking to many of us in the United States. That people might have to go without fresh water or live in the cold for months or years in our country is unthinkable.

The more functional a family is, the more they don't just "put food on the table." They are also knowledgeable about healthy and appropriate nutrition, healthy water, and clean air and are invested in upgrading these necessities when possible.

Health Needs Are Met

Children are properly immunized, allergies are tested and checked, strong and healthy teeth and bones are invested in, safety needs are seen to, checkups are done regularly, and sex education is properly conducted.

The more functional a family is, the better they do these things. This is another reason why poverty is violence. When families are deprived economically, they often cannot afford the costs, transportation, or other resources in people or time that it takes to get these necessary needs met in a complete and appropriate fashion. Lots of cash, on the other hand, does not mean that functionality will be automatic. Some well-to-do families can be just as neglectful as a family that lives with economic deprivation. Statistically, the odds are better that when a family is economically well off, the health needs of the children will be met.

Why is this important? First, if your body is in a suffering state, Maslow (1971) tells us that it is very difficult to pay attention to higher needs, such as achievement and creativity and being all that we can be (self-actualization). One's attention first and foremost, naturally goes to the toothache, the skin rash, the hunger in the stomach, or a less than desirable appearance, again and again. You cannot muster the concentration long enough for developing oneself to make it pay off—and development takes persistence. It is hard to persist at anything other than seeking relief when one is unhealthy.

It sends a not-so-subtle message of love to children when they see parents going to the extra lengths it takes to make sure they are healthy. Children may not send thank-you notes to parents for getting them braces or making sure the vitamin bottle is always full, but subconsciously, it is noticed and catalogued and, over time, sends a clear signal of care and support. One that says: "You are more than worthy of my sacrifices for you." For children, this builds an underlying confidence and sense of trust in the world.

When children who are well cared for grow up, they take care of their children the same way, establishing a healthy legacy of behaviors that are passed on. Healthy legacies in families are what build a strong country over time.

Problems Are Opportunities

Pertinent to this area of functionality, I witnessed two significant incidences within a week of each other that make the point perfectly. A movie director could not have staged them any better. Maybe these things happen because of coincidence, or perhaps I just notice them because I am a professor of learning psychology and a former psychotherapist.

The observational opportunity involved sitting in two different restaurants just a few days apart, but observing two similar situations that were handled very differently. Both involved a mom (there, but not part of the story), a dad, and a small daughter of about 4 years of age. I was eating alone nearby—typically, with a fork in one hand and a journal in the other—but in perfect proximity to view all aspects of these parallel situations. Both little girls accidentally knocked over their cups; one had juice in a small glass, the other milk.

When the first little tyke spilled her juice, the father went ballistic. "Now look what you have done!" He frantically grabbed a napkin, his tense body language similar to a military general moving alarmingly to stop the accidentally pushed red button from beginning a nuclear war. His face scowled at the little girl, and he huffed and puffed like the whole evening had just been ruined and it was her fault for not having finer muscle control. The look on her face was one of shame—sucked back in, with her lip quivering and her eyes going blank, as she had obviously learned to do many times before.

In the second situation, when the little girl spilled her small red plastic cup of milk, the father calmly looked over as the little girl began to get upset and began to reassure her, "That's okay, honey. These things happen." He smiled and picked up two paper napkins and gave her one. "Let's clean it up together," and again, "It's okay, sweetheart, it's just a little accident. We will get you another milk." Every kid should have such a dad.

The child in the second incident was actually the only one upset, and the father showed his stripes by making it a learning incident in several ways. One lesson, the obvious, is that accidents happen. It is what you do after the accident that counts. Second, the dad showed what a functional parent does in times of stress: comforts and reassures. Most important, he demonstrated that a delightful little girl's self-esteem was more important than the cost and mess of a spilled glass of milk or juice. Each time a parent physically or psychologically clobbers their kid over something, it sends an obvious message to them that *they* are worth less than *that*.

> What you live with you learn, what you learn you practice, what you practice you become.—Anthony Dallmann-Jones, from *Resolving Unfinished Business*

There are enough rough bumps in the road of life without a parent making more, and topping it off with a clear message: "If you can't count on me when you spill your juice, you can know that I will fumble the big ones that are sure to come your way. You are on your own, kid."

Maybe I am reading more into one or both situations than there was—and maybe less. But, regardless, the point is made that *life is problems—just one damn problem after another.* Whether it is taking time to refill the ice-cube tray when in a rush or leaving it for the next time (or person); whether to steer left or right when a deer runs in front of your car; whether to go to Yale or Harvard; whether an egg should be boiled quickly or slowly when making egg salad; and so on ad infinitum. Functional families help their children *prepare* for problems. They use problems as opportunities to teach various problem-solving techniques, decision making, handling emotions, prioritizing, and more, to build a child's confidence in their ability to handle life.

It's Okay to Make Mistakes

Dysfunctional families often lack the ability to effectively solve problems, so naturally, they dread their arrival because the family is just going to get weaker (more tired, more broke, more depressed) each time they pop up. And woe unto the family member who creates the problem by making a mistake. Mistakes are spotlighted and shamed in a misguided attempt to ward off the problem or prevent it from happening again. This is not unlike trying to kill a fly on the wall with a sledgehammer. It might work, but the damage caused is bigger than any benefit that might be reaped. Because there are always going to be mistakes where there are humans, a family where mistakes are not okay is a toxic environment because everyone is constantly trying to blame others for anything that goes wrong. Who wants to be hit with a sledgehammer?

If problems strengthen a functional family, then mistakes are critical to the growth of that family. Mistakes are seen as challenges, like a puzzle to be solved. Mistakes are seen as warning signals that we must take action to keep our family safe and healthy, so mistakes help stave off further danger and can easily have a positive spin to them. As a former certified diver who did some salvage work in the Gulf of Mexico, I was grateful for all the mistakes we made in training that gave our instructor an opportunity to remind us that you do not ascend faster than your bubbles or that you always carry a knife or that you never, ever dive alone. Our instructor was in the lifesaving business first and foremost. So are functional families.

Rides Easy in the Saddle

A dysfunctional family walks on thin ice. A functional family breaks the ice on purpose—sometimes just because. They can be spontaneous without fear. Functional families laugh. They smile. They can bear down seriously when needed, but can just get plain silly, too, because they know that one should not take oneself too seriously all the time in this life, because *life is to be enjoyed.* Life is not a crucifix. Life is not a jail sentence but, rather, a canvas to paint on, so why not paint it with fun and jubilation rather than with grayness and antagonism?

Dysfunctional families are so fear-based that they are constantly angry and/or depressed and/or tense, waiting for "the other shoe to drop." They cannot relax. They might buy relaxation tapes, but they get frantic when they can't find them.

Obviously, if a family does not have good problem-solving skills and if the next mistake just might be the proverbial straw that breaks the family's back, how can they be expected to hold the reins loosely? They either become hypervigilant, or out of exhaustion, they escape into something—anything—for relief, whether that might be excessive alcohol or drugs, television, tobacco, daydreaming, sex, shopping, gambling, eating, working, and so on. Anything to become unconscious.

CHAPTER 10

Life's Toolbox of Skills and Techniques

WITHIN the acorn is everything needed to grow the mighty oak tree, except external nourishment and some protection from the elements, until it is strong enough to withstand hardships on its own. If the seedling isn't nurtured by its environment, it dies or is stunted. This means that the tree may live, but it will have to endure the results of the deprivations it suffered as a seedling. This developmental plan is much the same for humans as well, no matter what the culture, ethnicity, or gender of the child.

At conception, we intrinsically possess all the things we need to achieve our full potential as wonderfully enlightened and fully developed beings. Our environmental requirement for these abilities to materialize is to be fully cherished. The supervisors of our environment are called *parents*. The ideal situation (which almost never happens) requires two very healthy parents to be fully developed as adults, spending most of their time raising the child until it can take care of itself, about two decades in our world today. This implies that the two parents themselves each had two such parents, and they each had two such parents. Unfortunately, the intergenerational legacies of abusive/neglectful child-raising, busy and/or preoccupied lifestyles, and the parents' own unfinished business rarely permit such a natural phenomenon to occur.

Utilizing the analogy of a toolbox, the child is born with all the tools necessary to achieve its rightful place in the world. Most of the tools are invisible at the time of birth. Some will acquire visibility naturally through healthy development, while others must be led out by caregivers. Some of the tools deal with emotions, some with communications, and others with interpersonal relationship skills, physical skills, problem-solving and decision-making skills, and so on. The list is very long, and the more tools you have, the greater your chances of success.

For example, suppose the primary caregiver doesn't know how to handle anger in a productive and healthy fashion. Children learn by example, and if the male child watches his father mishandle anger by pretending it isn't there, until one day he explodes over some seemingly trivial matter, how then would the child know differently except to handle his frustrations in this same "manly" fashion? It really isn't much different from parents not knowing how to use a hammer. For some reason (perhaps there is a belief that hammers are evil in this particular family tree), the children are taught to use a pair of pliers (a "pliers are good" legacy) to drive a nail. Pliers will get the job done, but won't be as effective or might hurt your fingers or damage the object that is being nailed. But they get you by. Sadly enough, this is exactly what many people do—get by—and believe that's all they deserve and maybe even feel lucky at that. But getting by is hardly why we exist. We know humankind has the potential to rise above the mere mastery of bodily needs and, indeed, choose to develop consciously.

Just how does the Shadow Child Syndrome prevent us from making increasingly progressive choices?

An Explanation

When a dry sponge is squeezed under water and released, the first molecules of water absorbed by the sponge go the deepest. When it is squeezed again those same first-in molecules will be the last to exit. Quite simply, this is one reason why parents are so powerful: *They are there first.* Their messages have more power in our lives because of a simple law of human physics: Two things cannot occupy the same space at the same time. The first message in (grained) concerning a certain topic has the most weight, healthy or not, productive or not. The message goes in, and there it stays with great resistance (inertia) to change, healthy or not, productive or not. This is because the human mind has one big operating need besides survival: *the need to be right.* The mind needs to be right about its conclusions, healthy or not, productive or not.

The need to be right is understandably necessary to function and survive. Deciding to cross the street you say to yourself, "It's okay to cross, right?" Without a responding "Right!" from within, you might remain standing indecisively on the corner forever. It is important to feel right about one's perceptions and decisions in order to move ahead with conviction in one's life. But, not unlike many life issues with dysfunctional family survivors, this need can become confused and often inappropriately applied.

Because of ineffective child-raising, our ego becomes warped with the need to be right, even to the point of self-destructive stubbornness, and indeed, many of us humans might be said to stubbornly die prematurely of "terminal righteousness." Normally we get by with justifying our perceptions of the world. We rationalize our shortage of tools and skills in a manner that allows us to be righteous, not only about our discomfort, but also about our unfulfilled destiny as fully potentialized human beings. We grow up honestly believing that life is hard, nice people finish last, and true happiness is probably (hopefully) achieved only after death. We even proclaim with T-shirts and bumper stickers such beliefs as "Life sucks, and then you die." These attitudes are perpetuated by the Shadow Child Syndrome in individuals. Also perpetuated are violence, mental illness, criminality, war, terrorism, continuances of child abuse and neglect, and much physical suffering and illness.

The only way to stop the ignorance and violence against the self and others in our families, schools, businesses, and society is by the following:

1. Understand exactly what constitutes abuse and neglect.
2. Refuse to perform, or enable, further harm.
3. Be able to accurately assess the appearance of Shadow Child Syndrome symptoms.
4. Institute programs that counteract, not just symptoms, but the underlying causative and perpetuating factors.

Dealing with symptoms is like locking the armory after the weapons are in the streets.—Joseph A. Califano, Former Secretary of Health, Education, and Welfare

Abuse, Neglect, and Susceptibility

The core issues to understand are *abuse, neglect,* and *human susceptibility.* Abuse is causing harm (the opposite of protection in the oak tree example), and neglect is lack of nurturing (nourishment in the oak tree example). Humans are particularly susceptible to the long-term effects of abuse and neglect because they are very sensitive, extremely intelligent, and highly adaptable.

Human Sensitivity

The component that makes people spiritual, empathic, caring, and capable of being supportive and compassionate has a downside; it also makes them vulnerable to the psychological after-effects of abuse and neglect. It goes with the territory that if one is going to care about others, one is also going to be exposed to potential injury. Compassion is a two-way street. As an example, in stress psychology research, the major stressors for an individual are created by loved ones and/or relatives. The paradox is that these are the same people (or positions) who can also fill a life with meaning, excitement, and love.

Worst case scenarios of people driven mad by abuse and neglect because of their sensitivity are those who internalize their world of activity, such as catatonics, and those who externalize their world of activity, such as antisocial personality types. Both internalizers and externalizers are reacting against their previous suffering, but in ways that destroy their ability to function in the "normal" world. When they are seen in this context, one realizes that one is watching victims in the process of reenactment, or doing unto self or others what was done unto them.

Human Intelligence

Humans are quick on the uptake. They usually don't have to be bitten more than once to get the message. Along with this quick-mindedness is the ability not only to remember events forever, either consciously or subconsciously, but to let those stored memories accumulate and affect future behavior. We call this ability learning. Children learn proportionately more the younger they are. In other words, someone who is 1 day old is learning more per waking hour than a 5 year old, who is learning more per waking hour than a 15 year old, who is learning more per waking hour than a 25 year old, and so on. Again, one of the very things that makes humans so special has a downside. The swinging door of human intelligence has *Tremendous Potential* written on one side, and *Damaged Easily* on the other side.

Worst case scenarios of people driven mad by abuse and neglect because of their intelligence are those who internalize with hallucinations and creative delusions and those who externalize with conniving, manipulating, or rapist mentalities.

One form of insanity is making the same mistake over and over and expecting different results.

Human Adaptability

Due in part to our intelligence, we humans are incredibly adaptive. We are able to adjust almost instantly to situations in order to get our needs met. This is especially true if we perceive a situation as one that may endanger our survival. This is exactly how abuse and neglect are perceived by the child, that is, as life threatening. Those in caregiver positions are the keepers of food, shelter, and, most of all, the affection that humans desperately need in order to develop appropriately and healthfully. Abuse and neglect are threats to the supply lines, and children intuitively know which side their bread is buttered on, especially when they are infants.

The sacrifice of the child's integrity with self occurs often and quickly and, at the time, seems a small price to pay to keep the supply lines open. In the long run, however, it can become another form of living death known as *codependence*. Extreme codependence is the externalized manifestation of someone driven mad to some degree because of haywired adaptability. The internalized form of adaptability gone sour is chronic anger and/or anxiety caused by a constant fear of losing control.

Addiction as Adaptation

Addiction is the inability to say "No" to an event, substance, or person that causes life-damaging consequences physically, mentally, emotionally, spiritually, socially, or financially. Addiction is a prominent adaptation that a person manifests internally and acts out externally in order to deal with the tear in their soul created by being raised in a dysfunctional environment. At one point in time, it seemed that alcoholism was the leading disease manifested by survivors of dysfunctional families. Later it was realized that all chemical dependencies were crutches in dealing with disease, and that alcoholism was just one form of drug addiction. This disease was finally titled "codependence" and it emerged into public awareness. It was realized that chemical addictions were just ways of dealing with the pain of living with the disease of codependence. In light of current knowledge, a deeper revelation is possible.

This book proposes that the major addiction in this world is the addiction to abuse. Although addictions are commonly seen as primary illnesses, they are not. Alcoholism, drug addiction, codependence, and others are just a means, or a vehicle, for the real illness: **The primary disease is a process addiction to abuse.** *It is a deep need to be steeped in abuse, whether that means receiving, dispensing, and attracting it.*

Hypothesis: Anyone with a less than nurturing family of origin easily develops a process addiction to some form of abuse, whether as a perpetrator, victim, or enabler.

Becoming Addicted to Abuse

The process addiction to abuse is a direct result of abuse/neglect in any form by primary caregivers, resulting in damage to the child's pristine self-esteem. This means that the child learned to disregard the true self and began to adapt by adopting a false self in order to be more pleasing to caregivers. This self-defeating adaptation is perpetuated through an inner drive to affirm subjective conclusions about reality through internal and external reenactments. The denigrating message that is learned and repeated to the self over and over is, *I am the kind of person who needs and/or deserves to be involved with abuse and/or neglect.* In order to be correct about this belief, the survivor attracts and creates a self-fulfilling flight plan of abuse and neglect in one or more of its many hydra-headed forms. Judging by the list in the Appendix I, there is no shortage of ways in which this prophecy can be self-fulfilled.

Without intervention, the means to abuse self and others physically, emotionally, mentally, or sexually are continually discovered by dysfunctional family survivors. There is also an attraction to affiliating with other "carriers" who become part of the drama. And it is a drama. It is not Nature's Plan, no matter how frequently it occurs and how normal it appears. We only need to remember Nazism to know that just because millions of people declare certain actions sane does not make them so.

Nature's Plan is evident when one observes a human baby born into a secure environment with a low-trauma delivery system. The baby is genuine: WYSIWYG (What You See Is What You Get). It is totally genuine and pure as an angel. Its skin even smells of sweetness. Its emotional expressions are exactly proportional to its interpretation of reality, not the reality of the person it has become codependent upon. The power of its purity will activate anyone around it.

We are tantalized by the newborn's ability to reflect, not unlike a mirror, our own unfinished family-of-origin business. If we were abused as an infant we may feel a need to hurt the child and/or modify its behavior so it won't be so genuine, that is, make it smile when it doesn't want to, make it stop crying because it bothers us, make it sleep when it apparently wants to be awake, make it eat when it isn't hungry, and so on. The infant has the need to survive like all of us and adapts to the tune of reinforcement, real or perceived. Thus it begins to abandon its *self*, and the pattern of abuse is formed. And, since we all do it, it appears quite normal.

But, of course, any untreated adult survivors around the baby don't really know what normal is—this is one of the major characteristics of the Shadow Child Syndrome.

The baseline premise behind all received abuse is that, *I am not acceptable as I am.* If I am being *abused* (a self-validated subjective experience) then I know I am not being cherished at this moment for what and who I am, and I feel mistrustful and ashamed. If this becomes a recurring pattern in my childhood, I develop a core of mistrust and shame. This core, not unlike plutonium rods (energizing but insulated and hidden) in nuclear reactors, becomes a toxic driving force, motivating destructive behavior inwardly (self-abuse) and/or outwardly (other-abuse). Because of its widespread nature, it can, indeed, become second nature. It infiltrates our families, our schools, our industry, and our institutions. It is highly contagious, spreading rapidly from person to person and generation to generation. A personality core of mistrust and shame is the fundamental cause of the Shadow Child Syndrome.

A fish swims up to another fish and says, "What do you think of this water today?" And the other fish replies, "What water?"

Is it possible that a child could only feel the world is normal when he or she is somehow involved with abuse or neglect? Yes, and reaching this state involves more than "getting used to it" or having it becoming a habit. It is much deeper than that. Because it was formed at such an early age, it establishes deep, subconscious roots that are nearly impossible to uproot. It *is* possible to uproot them, but only with serious therapy and a knowledgeable therapist—one who understands the psychodynamics of abuse and neglect. A therapist who has been in the inner jungle himself and has the tools and willingness to go there again with a client who is often anxious and perhaps in denial or resisting treatment. Most who have the process addiction to abuse do all they can to keep it, not knowing they have another choice.

CHAPTER 11

The Many Forms of Abuse

B REAKING the addictive cycle of abuse begins with awareness. Awareness is not always comfortable. Awareness of abuse is never comfortable. It is, however, necessary to become aware in order to break the vicious cycle. To paraphrase William Blake (1790): In order to escape from prison, the first thing you must do is realize that you are *in* one.

Towards a Nomenclature of Human Abuse and Neglect

In Appendix I there is a developed system for numbering/ categorizing the various forms of abuse and neglect. Professional educators, school counselors, social workers, and therapists are encouraged to use it in their field and discuss it with clientele and colleagues alike to spread its utility. There are several powerful rationales behind this attempt to classify. A main reason is that it may be the only method that can provide a language to communicate with people of judicial and legislative power in a way they can both relate and refer to with confidence.

The task was to develop a clarifying nomenclature, or definitive classification system, of abuse and neglect in order to encourage an accurate universal language for utilization by the public and professional sectors alike. This system greatly clarifies communications regarding traumatic incidents in people's lives. The goals accomplished by adopting a nomenclature are:

1. Universal recognition and agreement as to the exact practices, or behaviors, that are abusive/neglectful
2. Clear definition of the various forms of abuse/neglect

83

3. Establishment of a coded classification system for concise denotation and documentation

4. Provision of a foundation for the establishment of an accurate database for assessing the short- and long-term effects, including cost factors, of abuse/neglect on human beings

5. Creation of a set of standards on which to evaluate the current projected effectiveness of specific behaviors and practices utilized with children

6. Provision of an accurate assessment system by which society's health, education, legal, and human welfare agencies can make critical decisions affecting defenseless children and their future

With the standards set by the Classification System of Child Abuse and Neglect (CSCAN) in Appendix I, all of us have probably abused others, have allowed others to abuse us, and/or have abused ourselves. We are probably going to continue to do these things. The question is: Do we wish the abuse to increase, stay the same, or decrease in frequency? If we wish it to decrease, we must become more aware of all of the forms of abuse, including the subtle ones that we erroneously pass off as "harmless."

Definition of Abuse and Neglect

The CSCAN in Appendix I views abuse as an act of commission, and neglect as an act of omission. Despite the context commonly assumed and usually reinforced by the media that inflicting physical harm has more impact than any other form, what is more true is that the long-term psychological effects of both abuse and neglect are similar. Abuse is obviously overtly harmful, while neglect is, though covert, still damaging. It can be stated that neglect often creates more harmful effects because it is more difficult to identify and, therefore, not seen as the toxic agent that it is.

- *Abuse:* An act that is not accidental and harms, or threatens to harm, a person's physical, mental, or emotional health or safety
- *Neglect:* An act of omission that results, or could result, in the deprivation of essential services and/or goods necessary to maintain the minimum mental, emotional, or physical health of a person

Although not listed as a specific category in CSCAN, all abuse/neglect, no matter what form, is ultimately spiritual abuse because it facilitates the creating of a *false survivor-self.* This essentially manifests *a separation from the genuine self,* the main ingredient in the definition of spiritual abuse. One of the greatest tragedies of abuse and neglect is that survivors wander through life never knowing who they really are. Without intervention, they cannot find their way home to a restored sense of true self.

It is suggested that the reader turn to Appendix I to view the CSCAN before proceeding.

Section III

The Shadow Children Syndrome:
The Inside Story

CHAPTER 12

The Shadow Child Syndrome

THE Shadow Child Syndrome is a condition that occurs as a direct result of being raised by anyone other than nurturing caregivers. Children develop any of the following eight personality traits in order to survive abusive and/or life-threatening environments. Shadow Children carry these adaptation traits through their growing years and often unnecessarily into adult lives that are limited by these same strategies. More often these traits in adulthood are legitimized in various ways rather than being seen as pieces of handicapping, unfinished business. Having thus been rationalized, they go unaddressed and are easily perpetuated across and down through many family layers. In other words, this life-strangling insidiousness can become an accepted part of a family's legacy to its children for many generations.

In a subsequent chapter, we will look at these eight characteristics of the Shadow Child Syndrome again in light of the educational environment. Although these eight are always present, they manifest themselves differently in different environments. Because of the intensity of schools, (remember just how intense school environments are for children) symptoms of the syndrome often are exhibited sideways or they are camouflaged. The Shadow Child is the proverbial wolf in sheep's clothing.

Survivor Traits of Shadow Children

Control Consciousness

Growing up in unstable and unpredictable environments creates chaotic inner feelings and uncertainty (American Medical Association

1995). One learns to be watchful and cautious in order to survive. One learns to control emotions, thoughts, and behaviors through suppression and denial, hoping this will help control the self, others, and the world (English, Widom, and Brandford 2004). One feels he or she must have some control in order to have predictability in an unpredictable world (Woititz 1987). Violations of the child during Erikson's Trust vs. Mistrust Stage (from birth to 1 year of age) create such a mistrust of the world as a safe place that control seems necessary in order to survive.

Avoiding Emotions

The dysfunctional training that children receive instills a denial of their feelings: "Don't trust any of your emotions to benefit you, and ignore what your senses tell you" (Seixas 1985). When adults show emotion it is often associated with abusive situations, and children assume a direct cause and effect relationship (Fischer et al. 1992). The message is, "Don't trust others and their emotions, and don't trust your own emotions either" (Farmer 1989).

Inability to Grieve to Completion

Especially noteworthy of dysfunctional family survivors is their inability to grieve losses to completion (Farmer 1989). The "tunnel of grief" has four sequential stations: (1) shock and denial, (2) anger and/or fear/bargaining, (3) sadness, and (4) acceptance and/or gratitude. Inability to grieve means that with each need-to-let-go situation, one gets stuck in one of the stations and never reaches the stage of acceptance. Changes are constant in life. With each change usually comes a death, whether it is leaving the first grade for the second, quitting cigarettes, letting go of one's youth, quitting a relationship, or leaving home. Inability to grieve to completion means that there are many Shadow Children in perpetual states of shock, denial, anger, fear, and/or sadness.

Guilt from Overresponsibility

The guilt carried in the core of the dysfunctional family survivor stems from feeling overly responsible for caretakers' actions and feelings (Woititz 1987). The Shadow Child may even feel guilty for the abuse suffered and perhaps for any punishment that siblings received.

Shadow Children carry to school and into eventual adulthood the habitual and overwhelming pattern of feeling the need to be a caretaker to others (Farmer 1989). Whether they do it or not is another thing, but if they do not act it out, then they will *act it in*. This means that they will internalize the lack of action as feelings of guilt and inadequacy. Either way, no matter how much caretaking they actually do or don't do, it will never be enough. That is because this is compulsive behavior, and with compulsive behavior, as Janet Woititz (1994) aptly states: "If what you want is not what you need, it will never be enough."

Crisis Addiction

Inconsistencies, surprises, and terror perhaps were the norm in the childhood of Shadow Children, so when things are calm and stable, Shadow Children may feel deadened or bored, thereby necessitating an urge to stir things up (Whitfield 1984). Although they may complain outwardly about chaos, Shadow Children may be uncomfortable deep inside when it is not present. Some Shadow Children develop an excitement addiction, and will generate an uproar game if things are too serene. Often, this appears as sabotage in school, business, or relationships. *They just can't stand success* might be a phrase that can apply to some Shadow Children.

Guessing at Normality

What is normal? Since the home lives of most dysfunctional family survivors' were extremist in nature, no standards were established for the concept of normality. As they grow, Shadow Children are constantly confused as to what is really healthy and normal (Woititz 1987). They frequently feel unsure inside, although they may have complex strategies to portray themselves as otherwise (Crespi 1995).

Low Self-Esteem

Being abused and neglected delivers the message, "You are not good enough the way you are." When self-adjusting brings the same response again, one perceives, "The truth is that no matter what I do, I am not good enough" (Teicher 2000). Thus, the core of shame overshadows the pristine self, and Shadow Children regard themselves as defective or irretrievably damaged. It is impossible to develop a benevolent self-concept in this soil. Shadow Children find many ways to reaffirm the belief that they are, indeed, always "less than" in thoughts, words, and actions (Steinglass 1987). It is this self-validating, internalized assumption that delivers the crucifying mandates by which Shadow Children often shape their lives (Wegscheider-Cruse 1989).

Compulsive Behaviors

One of the earliest evaluative scales we all learned as infants was pain versus pleasure. Human beings avoid pain and seek pleasure. The psychological pain of being alienated from the true self is one of the most intense, confusing, and enduring possible. It resembles an incurable migraine of the soul (Whitfield 1984). Compulsive behavior of any sort offers an irresistible anesthesia for the psychological pain as well as a pleasant diversion for the body. One can be compulsive about almost anything: alcohol and other drugs, work, gambling, food, shopping, hoarding, sex, exercise, relationships, religion, particular emotion look-alikes (rageaholism, sadaholism, phobias), power, money, violence, and so on ad infinitum (Kellogg 1990).

The Shadow Child Syndrome and Limits and Boundaries

If one could locate an underlying theme of the eight characteristics of the Shadow Child Syndrome, it would be about distorted external and internal limits and boundaries. *Limits* are self-determined lines in the sand of how far I am going to let myself go, such as "I am only going to eat 2000 calories today," "I am going to quit work at noon today," or "I am not going to loan you any more money." *Boundaries* are self-determinations about how far I am going to let you go, such as "You cannot talk to me like that," "Don't come over to my house without calling first," "If you hit me I will call the police," "Don't ask me that anymore" and so on.

The simplest definition of a good upbringing is one where a child learns to healthfully set limits and boundaries in such a way as to prosper physically, mentally, emotionally, socially, and spiritually for the rest of their life. Dysfunctional upbringing wreaks havoc with this important ability. As an exercise in this, review the eight Shadow Child Syndrome characteristics and interpret them with *limits* and *boundaries* in mind.

Recovery, Uncovery, and Discovery

Recovery is the process of working to uncover the natural self so there might be restoration to a balanced way of life. In this way, the Shadow Child (whether still a child or grown up) can enjoy being true to his/her and others' genuine selves. Recovery is often accomplished through 12-step groups, counseling, and support groups, which are all various means of personally resetting limits and boundaries. Sometimes more concentrated recovery work is necessary, such as therapeutic treatment, rehabilitation, and/or medication, which are all means of having structured limits and boundaries established for the individual. A general rule of thumb is that the more intense the abuse and neglect was then, the more intense the recovery work will have to be now.

John Bradshaw—along with Terry Kellogg—ushered into prominence the recovery field for survivors of abusive/neglectful families in the mid 1980s. In his 1988 book, *Healing the Shame That Binds You,* Bradshaw brought the topic of recovery for survivors of abuse and neglect into mainstream American awareness with an eight-part series that aired on PBS. The series was centered around the need for healing (recovery), whether you knew you needed it or not. The series was used as a PBS fundraiser and John was the hottest speaker going. Few knew that a lot of his work was based on experiences he learned at the feet of Terry Kellogg, a genius of a man who dedicated his life to recovery work and cared little about receiving credit for his work. Terry appeared in two of the series parts with John and made famous the definition of passive-aggressive behavior as: "A Saint Bernard licking you on the face and peeing on your leg at the same time."

One part of the process of recovery that each of these men wrote about in the beginning was to differentiate exactly what recovery was. (Read either of their books on this: Kellogg's *Broken Toys, Broken Dreams* or Bradshaw's *Healing the Shame That Binds You.*) In *Healing the Shame That Binds You,* Bradshaw defines three areas or zones for overcoming the harmful effects of being raised in a dysfunctional family: recovery, uncovery, and discovery. Though catchy, these three words represent accurate concepts.

Recovery

Recovery is often and erroneously seen as the end goal of overcoming an addiction (i.e., quitting drinking). As most successful recovering alcoholics/addicts will tell you, they started out truly believing that if your drug of choice is alcohol, then drinking too much of it was their problem. Once the alcoholic or drug abuser had the courage to admit it, the next thing to do was quit drinking or using. Most of them, if they abstained long enough, came to see that chemical addiction was not cured by abstention alone. Overdrinking might be cured by not drinking, but not drinking did not heal alcoholism. Alcoholism and drug addiction is, as the expression goes, "a way of thinking, not a way of drinking."

Drinking too much alcohol is a symptom of something much deeper. Drinking too much can become habit-forming, and once it does it calls for more and more alcohol. The old saying, "One day a thousand drinks is not enough, and one is too many," bears this out, and calls for something deeper than cessation. That next and deeper level is called *uncovery*.

Because stopping an addiction to alcohol consumption is such a monumental task in and of itself, it is easy to see how one could believe that cessation is enough to ask of the alcoholic. It *is* asking a lot. There are an estimated 4,000,000 habitually excessive drinkers in the United States. Twenty-five percent of them are alcoholics. Among them, 15 percent will, at some point, fully stop drinking (Becker 2008). This means that just 0.0375, or 3.7 percent, of excessive drinkers stop drinking.

Actually, abstinence is just the first of three steps, with each step containing several sub-steps. The goal of all alcoholics/addicts is to protect their supply. Recovery involves stopping drinking *and* surrendering all of the defensive behaviors that keep people "away from your supply," such as power plays and controlling techniques, rage attacks, self-pity, grandiosity, perfectionism, blaming and shaming others, and seeing oneself as a victim. In other words, recovery can keep you busy for quite awhile. If you start using again you will have to start over from the beginning, *if* you manage to recover (again). There is always another binge, but not always another recovery.

Uncovery

If the addict is willing, at some point the uncovery phase will occur. If not, you are usually seen as a "white-knuckler"—one who grits his teeth and counts the days since last drinking/using. Uncovery is, as the name implies, an uncovering of all the submerged and forgotten things that led to addiction as an anesthetic in the first place. This can be a long phase of shedding denial, letting go of the need to play a role in the family of origin, and letting go of addiction (Black 1981). Those who are addicted to alcohol and other chemicals have often become very attached to the role of "hero" or "victim" or "the offender" or "the scapegoat" or "the mascot/jester" or "the lost child." Each of these roles have at least one thing in common—they alleviate pain. All compulsive behaviors and addictive substances have the following two attributes: They give the user a little shot of joy and a bit of anesthesia at the same time. This is a hard combination to beat, and many large businesses are centered on making sure we never forget those advantages. Tobacco, alcohol, and junk-food companies are such businesses that come to mind.

Discovery

Whether you like Sigmund Freud's concepts or not, we must pay homage to a man who was the first to explain the concepts of repression, denial, and suppression, and other means of protecting our "shame core" (Bradshaw 1988). Freud called them *primary process defense mechanisms*. They exist to protect human beings from one another. This has to be true because they do exist, and they only exist because we have relationships. If I was born on a planet and the only person alive, why would I need psychological protection? Freud authored volumes on what happens inside us because we cannot be affirming one another 100 percent of the time. Is all of Freud's work valid?

For our purposes it is important to note that we do suppress and repress things, we do deny truth and hide things from one another, and these practices do trip us up from having a full, rich, and healthy life—sometimes. But let us remember our purpose here: We are looking at how and what children project and hide that encourages them to *act out in the school environment,* and what a knowledgeable authority figure can do about it. Obviously the first step is to learn what is going on inside that young person, and how manifesting behaviors can be channeled productively. *Channeled.* This is a deliberate choice of words. Human beings cannot stop behavior, because we are made of molecular action that is always on the move. If we stop, we die. My point is that as informed adults we have learned to shift a child away from destructive/non-productive behaviors and channel them towards healthy, productive ones.

Reaching the Core

Survivors of abusive/neglectful families have heard one message over and over: "You are not good enough the way you are." Sometimes a child is told it, sometimes they feel it, and sometimes the message comes in the form of abuse and neglect that always contains the message that you are not okay the way you are. The more dysfunctional the family, the more persistent and frequent this message is delivered. When a child grows up with this message internalized, they begin to believe it, and then they begin to act it out. Negative, disrespectful, critical, and angry verbal behaviors are often a way of exhibiting that they believe it. We as parents, educators, authority figures, and youth workers may not know what to do, but we should at least know this: We do not want to pour gasoline on the fire in an attempt to put it out! Schools are often based on a *deficiency model* of constantly telling the child he or she is low in this, short in that, insufficient at this, and poor at that. All this does is reinforce the child's false belief that he or she is unlovable, undesirable, and unwanted. And the child will begin to redouble their efforts to prove that it is true. Human beings often show they would rather be right than almost anything else, even it if the thing to be right about is unpleasant and/or uncomfortable.

In the next chapter, we will look more closely at what happens in the school environment as the Shadow Child Syndrome is activated in the classrooms and hallways. The next chapter explains implications of the Shadow Child Syndrome for the most popular institution in the United States: Education. This chapter is a shortened version of what could (and has) taken up volumes. The purpose is to quickly give the reader a flavor of (1) how the Shadow Child Syndrome looks in action, and (2) some insights that might show strategic intervention possibilities.

A special acknowledgment goes to my good friend Dr. Steven Farmer for his pioneering work in the recovery field, and for his assistance in developing the dysfunctional family survivor characteristic list that led to the Shadow Child Syndrome. Steven is a psychotherapist from Laguna Beach, California and the author of four books: *The Wounded Male, Adult Children of Abusive Parents, Healing Words,* and *Sacred Ceremonies.*

CHAPTER 13

Implications of the Shadow Child Syndrome in the Educational Environment

CHILDREN bring their unfinished business to school in pencil and lunch boxes, and educators bring their unfinished business in briefcases. At the starting bell everyone snaps open their respective containers and starts throwing the contents at each another. It lasts all day. It wears everyone out and is usually given the general title of *discipline problem.* Due to misidentification and ignorance, nothing ever gets resolved, things can even be made worse and, most often, everyone becomes frustrated, resentful, and depressed. Usually, the most creative response to all the expanding symptomologies is that the school policy manuals get thicker every year. The first Shadow Child Syndrome symptom, *control consciousness,* is ironically never more obvious than in the educational environment.

Control Consciousness

Schools are mostly about control. Can the kids control their urges and learn to delay gratification? Can the teachers control themselves enough so that they will be the kind of educational technicians that can create that magical thing known as the learning environment? Can the administrators control their images, energy levels, budgets, and staff in order not to look bad and yet still carry out the edicts created by the federal government, state legislature, state department of education, local school board, public, parents, business leaders, changing times, and so on?

A trained family systems therapist can walk through a school and, after listening to a few minutes of several conversations and watching the corresponding body language, interpret for you a whole universe of the unfinished family business that lurks behind most interactions in the school. It's mostly about fear—the fear of losing control. Although the therapist's interpretation will be correct, no one will want to hear it and, most likely, it will either be derided or promptly ignored. This is because the interpretation is right on the money, and as the old saying goes: The truth hurts.

Every year, our schools are becoming bigger and bigger catch basins of unfinished family of origin business influencing every person in them. To be honest with you, I personally wouldn't teach in a school today unless the staff was aware of this. Dysfunction is most dangerous when denied, meaning that additional dysfunctionality is going to be perpetrated because denial is occurring. This is what we mean by a "highly toxic environment." In their ignorance and denial, some professionals are treating poison victims with bigger doses of poison. And it's all done in a futile effort to heal the pain, or at least control it. One of the goals of researching and publishing these findings is to halt the process of naively trying to put out fire with gasoline.

Control Modalities for Children

It is natural for healthy children to want to learn, grow, and develop. We assume the school environment and its personnel are encouraging this development. But what if the child is blocked from natural progress by dysfunctional control mechanisms learned in a dysfunctional home? How might we identify those modalities in Shadow Children?

Retreat Modality

Passivity, shyness, withdrawing, phobias, anxiousness, fearfulness, and "spiritual limpness" are various expressions of someone suffering from a general mistrust of their environment. For that person, life has perhaps become a series of abusive/neglectful episodes, and the best strategy is to run as far away as possible. It makes sense to avoid uncomfortable things, but the reaction of the Shadow Child will appear odd as the threat isn't apparent in the school environment, but it is very real inside the person. We must remember that we carry our historical universe with us in our internal microclimate, and *that* is where we react from. Think of these Shadow Children as having retreated into the recesses of a cave as far as they can go. It's lonely and damp in there, but it appears safer than what masquerades as life-giving sunlight outside the cave. In what way could you reassure these cave dwellers that they could dare take the risk to come out and try once more to develop? Once you get them out, what would you have to do to sustain that trust? (See also The Tunnel of Grief section later in this chapter.)

Aggressive Modality

A good offense is the best defense. Sound familiar? This is a fairly accurate truism in our world today. Its roots are in childhood. Let's be honest, we admire someone who fights back, who stands up after being abused, and growls, "Enough!" Why don't we admire this spunk in kids? Because it's often misplaced. They can't fight their abusers and neglectors. Either they don't know who the abusers are because the abuse was camouflaged or justified, or it's too dangerous to confront the offender. (Did you stand up and growl at your parents when they cracked you one or called you names, or did you take it out on someone else/yourself?)

What do these children need? Acknowledgment of their wounds, a chance to heal them and, ideally, training in how to creatively express their pain. They will also desperately need to learn from a healthy model how to set limits and boundaries for themselves in society. Schools have an excellent opportunity to teach (and be) this model. Democracy must be reinvented every generation. The general environmental rule in school should be this: "We will give you educational opportunities to set your own healthy limits and boundaries, but if you can't we will do it for you until you can. Our goal is to help you learn how to healthfully self-monitor and self-adjust your life toward quality outcomes."

Mental Illness Modality

Few mental patients come from functional homes. Children with mental illness are unconsciously trying (unsuccessfully and unhealthfully) to fill a need. Mental illness is a means of controlling either the external or internal environment to reduce threat or pain. It may show up in the forms of obsessive behaviors, dissociation, depression, self-abuse, violence, chemical abuse, and/or anti-social behaviors. If an educator knows that the root of the aberrant behavior is a lost child trying to cope, they can more easily endure the child's search to find him or herself in their darkness. The educator can be a friend with a flashlight who is leading the child to either healthier patterns or to someone who can teach them healthier patterns. A professional educator knows their sources for referral.

Overachieving or Underachieving Modality

Trying to be more than you are is self-abusive, and trying to be less than you are is self-abusive. A healthy life includes acceptance of the self as a developing entity with a potentially great, although unknown, future, and feeling good about that. Kids who dramatically over- or undershoot their academic targets are often trying to prove themselves to be somebody they are not and unconsciously using the curriculum as a vehicle of self-abuse. Be suspicious of students who look miserable (anxious, sad, frantic) no matter how much they overachieve, and students who look too satisfied with underachieving.

Avoiding Emotions

If children aren't emotions, what are they? If humans aren't emotions, what are we? But children are supposed to "let it out." Having emotions is a major facet of being a human being, and children manifest this quite obviously. Part of being "childish" is allowing those emotions to rise to the surface and displayed quite obviously. One comical view of school is to see it as a bunch of little emotional agendas running up against a bunch of totally emotionless curriculum guides, policy manuals, and schedules. In actuality, this is more of a tragedy than a comedy because it occurs in schools on a daily basis. Shadow Children coming from dysfunctional environments often exhibit a twisted approach to their own emotions, what they are, and how to express and resolve them appropriately.

Q: What is the school's response to children's emotions?
A: A good day is when children have no emotions and just quietly do their work.

Q: What should the school's response be?
A: Emotions are neither good nor bad but are responses to the environment, and they have an onset, sequence, and an end. They are indicators of what we love or fear and, as such, indicate our values. There are healthy ways to experience and benefit from your emotions. Let us accept emotions as a normal part of the day and show students how to effectively handle their emotions as part of the curriculum.

Inability to Grieve

I have listened to adult clients showing little emotion as they offer up a laundry list of abuses heaped upon them as children. When finished, I would ask them what they did *not* get as children that they wished they would have gotten, and that was when the hurt and tears began to show. Almost everyone felt ashamed to admit that they felt betrayed, ripped off, or denied what we all need as children: a healthy, loving, safe, and nurturing family that accepts—no, affirms—us exactly as we are. The shame, via an unwarranted sense of a seemingly sinful selfishness, felt by these adult survivors is what blocks the grief work that is necessary to finally lay to rest a childhood full of heartbreak.

It is not possible to grieve to completion if you feel that you do not have a right to feel that way, if what you feel is "unearned" (e.g., if in the commission of a felony you lose your right arm most people would agree you have no right to feel bad about losing your arm). Many abuse/neglect survivors feel that it is their fault they have been mistreated (i.e., if I had not been so much of a burden to my family I would not have been hurt so much by my caregivers). Survivors of abuse and neglect often feel like family felons. Children are easily and quickly convinced of their evilness and the trouble they put their parents through: "We were poor, then You came along!"

The Tunnel of Grief

Children in school exhibit their unfinished grief work in a number of ways. If one looks at the "tunnel of grief" that one must go through to fully accept any separation, it facilitates an understanding of where children might get stuck.

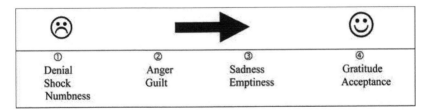

①	②	③	④
Denial	Anger	Sadness	Gratitude
Shock	Guilt	Emptiness	Acceptance
Numbness			

It is helpful if we empathize with children (or anyone) who is suffering a loss. In some ways, when we empathize is when we are most human. We can productively learn about the tunnel of grief by utilizing our own experiences. Take a moment and clearly remember a past separation, one that you are not comfortable with. It could be a death; a loss; a separation from a person, place, or job; a phase of life; or a behavior. Think about this still painful or unfinished separation for a moment, and then reflect: "In which stage of grief am I still stuck?" (It helps to take slow, deep, and relaxed breaths while doing this.)

- *Stage 1—Shock/Denial/Numbness:* Are you still numb? Do you say, "I can't bear to think about it"? Do you have difficulty remembering it? Does it seem hazy, faint, or far away? Does your mind have trouble staying focused on that past separation?
- *Stage 2—Anger/Guilt:* Are you resentful? Do you feel cheated or ripped off? Could it be that you really need to feel anger but won't let yourself because it may appear trivial, selfish, silly, futile, or undeserved? Or do you feel angry at yourself (guilt) for not doing all you feel you should have done?
- *Stage 3—Sadness/Emptiness:* Are you depressed about it? Feel the need to cry about it? Inconsolable? Hurt? Empty? Lost? Lonely? Exhausted?
- *Stage 4—Gratitude/Acceptance:* Do you see how you benefited from the experience, person, or thing from which you are now separated? Do you feel peaceful or pleasant when you remember? Do you have insight as to how that experience/person/thing has helped you to cope better with your life today? If so, you have at least made an initial journey all the way through the tunnel of grief.

Know that, if the separation was highly traumatic, you may need to go through the tunnel for the same event more than once in order to peel away the internal layers of the tunnel. It is comforting to know that each layer is easier and faster than the previous one. One day, when you have completely "cored out" the tunnel, it will vanish, leaving wisps of nostalgia and gratitude in your mind.

There are four helpful things to remember while in the middle of the grieving process: (1) any loss—whether it seems warranted or not—needs to be grieved; (2) it is natural, healthy, and necessary to grieve the many separations we must pass through in our lifetime; (3) it is helpful to breathe in nice slow circles with a relaxed exhale when experiencing grief (this allows the body to surrender to the truth of your emotions); and (4) know in your heart that this pain is temporary—that it *does* pass, contrary to the feelings that make it seem endless.

The grief process is about becoming honest and taking responsibility for our emotional lives. Successful grief work liberates us from our past, allows us to ride easy in the saddle of the present, and promotes enthusiasm about our ability to handle whatever the future may bring.

Back to our major point: We may discover kids in various stages of grief at any time. Students who are called airheads or daydreamers or unconscious are probably in the first stage of grief and don't know how to move past it. They are in shock, denial, or just numb from the experiences of abuse/neglect. Angry kids have been denied the love that they need and are feeling ripped off. Sad children are experiencing the void or a seemingly endless sea of emptiness.

By accepting feelings as legitimate, a professional educator can help move children through the stages to gratitude and acceptance so they can get to a proactive state of being naturally in the moment and can begin to rebuild their lives in a manner deserved from the beginning. If an educator feels awkward or insecure doing this they should refer the child to a counselor. Not tomorrow. Today. Why? I would hazard a guess that almost every teen suicide is precipitated by unresolved grief work.

Guilt from Overresponsibility

Probably the saddest children to witness are the ones who try to become little adults too soon. It is an impossible goal, but they do all they can to become that adult as early as possible. Why? It is the way some children get approval and attention. It may be that the child has fallen into the pattern and is compulsive about it in order to mask or anesthetize some psychological conflict or pain. They are trained like dogs to be little servants by their caregivers. "Fetch this." "Fetch that." "Good boy!"

Unfortunately, we often mistakenly call these children good because they more than likely become overachievers or even little helpers for the teachers. It is important to look behind the scenes here and make sure that we are not enabling an already unhealthy pattern. Children are not supposed to be developing such broad shoulders when they have such little bones. If this is not discouraged, Shadow Children will grow up into classic enablers themselves. They will guilt their own children for not being constantly productive little worker bees. The legacy is quite viral: "You were not born to have a good time; you were born to produce!" A normal, good life is balanced. There is work and there is play—and one is not more holy than the other.

Guilt is all about breaking rules or standards. The guilt-ridden statement "I am not a good person" means that I have not lived up to the standards of goodness. But just whose standards of goodness have I internalized, and are they clear, healthy, and appropriate? Children trying to grow up too fast are often attempting to be surrogate parents or even spouses in the name of "goodness." This easily taints or even kills the precious flower of childhood.

Crisis Addiction

Kamikaze kids look like they can't stand success. Just when things are starting to go well, Shadow Children screw it up. (Please note, some Shadow Children act *out* and others act *in*, but these are just two sides of the same coin. They are *acting a symptom* either way.) If this applies to a child in your life or school environment, then know that this is the symptom being played out. Some Shadow Children feel electrically alive only during a crisis. Other Shadow Children have adopted a strategy of crisis-creation to get a semblance of affection, although it may look like they just want attention. Negative attention, for some children, is better than none at all, much like having bad breath is better than having no breath at all. These children need to be shown more appropriate paths to getting their needs met. They need positive attention when things are calm, or a means of getting affection without playing the uproar game.

Guessing at Normality

How could kids coming out of some of the homes they do have even an approximation of what the concept of *normal* means? They have been in a pool of such craziness and abuse/neglect that their standards of normalcy are either warped or nonexistent. They have mostly been trying to survive, not worrying about acceptable social standards. The school must model sanity and a limits-and-boundaries system based on an established range of acceptable normalcy. I repeat: Democracy must be reinvented every generation. Children usually must rely on the school to learn the wonderful system of concern for peers, built on the Three Musketeers slogan, "All for one and one for all!" If the school cannot establish this productive counterculture for a child, then all is usually lost for that particular individual. Fair or not, the school is often the last bastion for teaching sane and healthy social interaction.

If the school itself is a poor example, then the only safety net left for these children is a life of institutions, prisons, or death (living or otherwise).

Low Self-Esteem

Shadow Children, like everyone else, are born with naturally healthy (some call this high) self-esteem; however, it becomes covered over with environmental pollution in a dysfunctional family. The school's function is to provide a counteracting force where children can prove to themselves that they deserve the self-esteem that they were born with. Unfortunately, out of pure ignorance, the school system often unwittingly revictimizes the victim. Schools, although they should know better by now, still naively expect children to come to school with all their "oars in the water." When the kids don't fit the expectations of the curriculum guides or normed behavioral standards for their grade levels, they are then seen as little cognitive deficits and are either discarded or patronizingly labeled and treated like moronic cattle—none of which serves to uncover the healthy self-esteem that needs to be expressed.

Success is the greatest esteem-builder. If an educational system is so deficiency-based (always looking for what is missing rather than what is present) that it is unaware of constantly sending the all too familiar message to the child: "Oh, and another thing wrong with you is . . ." then it becomes a collaborator in the soul-killing system already established for the child by his or her dysfunctional home environment.

Compulsive Behaviors

For ease of explanation, I want to lump addictive and compulsive behaviors together. Let us just agree that we are discussing children who are into destructive cycles of behaviors or habits that they cannot say "No" to. Again, compulsive-addictive behaviors are actually a form of mental illness, but many of them have become acceptable, even seen as normal, by large parts of our society (Dube et al. 2001). We easily become blind to these toxic "habits" because, as classic dysfunctional members of the bigger societal family ourselves, we have developed a high tolerance for inappropriate behavior and pain. But just because we have gotten used to cigarette smoking, alcohol consumption, work addiction, gambling, hypo- and hyper-eating problems, relationship addictions, and more does not take away their destructive impact on society or its Shadow Children.

A healthy school environment, by definition, must establish a confrontative (truth-telling) attitude toward self-destructive behaviors and, if it has the resources, provide support for recovery from such behaviors. Here is where good role-modeling, school support groups, school counselors and psychologists, and satellite social services pay off. Compulsive-addictive behavior patterns are tough to break because they give a little shot of pleasure along with a lot of temporary relief from pain. This explains why they are so prevalent. The countermeasures have to be commensurately healthy and determined enough for the fight that will last the long haul. *Confrontation does work,* as statistics have shown in systems that have targeted specific, destructive patterns with hard-hitting programs. Always expect a fight. Nobody wants to give up their pain-killing placebo because it feels like the only life raft on the ocean to them. The answer is to provide a more attractive raft.

Conclusion

This has been a very abbreviated covering of the eight behavioral categories of the Shadow Child Syndrome. Remember that a *syndrome* is a number of symptoms that, when grouped together, help identify a disease or "condition" that may have eluded our understanding. In our case, the Shadow Child Syndrome has been established to assist educators in identifying and explaining behaviors exhibited by abused and neglected survivors who still—if they survive—come to school. Remember, four children a day die in the United States from abuse and/or neglect. Many of them did not make it to school age. The rest were in front of an educator at one point—then never seen again. What kind of educator does it take to be ready to play that key role in changing a young life for the better?

We know what kind does not.

You do not have to be in public education very long until you land in front of a Mr. Hollenbacher.

Mr. Hollenbacher was a curmudgeon. If you look it up in the dictionary, you will find Hollenbacher's picture next to the word. It seems that every high school faculty in the country has had one assigned to it. Every committee has to have a chair, and every faculty has to have at least one curmudgeon. Our pet curmudgeon was a business teacher who was 2 (long) years away from retirement. Next to smoking a pipe and reading the *Wall Street Journal,* one of Mr. H's favorite self-appointed job assignments was to deliver his private orientation speech to new faculty in the teachers lounge at the earliest opportunity, each school year.

Although barely 22 years old and with a still-wet diploma signature, I can still remember his succinct and fairly vivid speech. Similar to Foghorn Leghorn, the cartoon rooster with the booming voice, Mr. Hollenbacher would clear his throat and point his pipe stem at the intended recipient of his one pearl of wisdom: "You can take my word for it or not, but I have been teaching in this school for 40 years and am—Thank God!—only 2 years from retirement, knock on wood. Here's what you do. You take your losers, greasers, and knuckleheads and stick them in the back of the room. You tell 'em, 'I don't care what you #@&*'s do—sleep, read comic books, or draw cartoons—but you shut the #@&* up and don't bother me or anyone else in this GD room. Okay? Are we clear?' Then you teach to the front rows—the kids who really want to learn. That's the secret."

Click. The pipe stem went back between the teeth.

Snap. The *Wall Street Journal* popped back up in front of his face.

Thus endeth the lesson.

For each Mr. Hollenbacher there are hundreds of caring, earnest, professional educators. But they are not as a confident about what they should be comprehending, or what could be done with "those kids" as the Mr. Hollenbachers are. Mr. Hollenbacher seemed so knowledgeable and authoritative. He wore a snappy suit every day. The rest of us had khaki slacks, loafers, and two or three sport coats. I personally had no idea what all those complicated columns of microscopic information in the *Wall Street Journal* were trying to say, but it looked very important, and he understood it. The loudest squeak gets the grease. Usually. But not always.

At-risk kids need loud protectors, not rejecters. They did not ask to be placed at risk any more than they asked to be abused or neglected. Why are there Mr. Hollenbachers within our ranks? They are school-children haters. They mock them, deride them, scare them, do all they can to make them feel at fault for being who they have been made to be. How can we even allow people like this in our fine profession? The first day a professional begins to act like this should also be his or her last day on the job. Just like a lawyer who comes into the lawyers lounge and says, "I threw that case, lowlife scum client!" or the doctor who enters the doctors lounge and says, "I made her sicker! Ha-ha. Pathetic patients! I am sick of them . . . ha-ha-ha . . . sick of them—get it? I crack me up." These people are not funny or clever. They are a blight on their profession and should be weeded out quickly.

As a profession, we educators will look back one day and wonder why we did not see the Shadow Children sooner and better, and implement smart and caring intervention plans sooner and better. Perhaps it is because we did not have the knowledge we needed to match our willingness to help. Hopefully, the succinct and vivid descriptions of the various aspects of the Shadow Child Syndrome will bring us closer to the confidence that is needed to proceed with the intervention strategies necessary to rescue these children who, but for us, would have no other champions in their lives.

Section IV

Prevention and Intervention:
Where It Should All Begin . . .

CHAPTER 14

At-Risk Program Considerations

THERE is no established, distinctive success formula for an at-risk program. The formulae vary dramatically across the country. Some programs have failed, and some have succeeded. Most are in-between, muddling along—losing some kids, getting others through the system. There has either been enough success with pullout programs for at-risk students or enough desperation and frustration with at-risk students in the traditional classrooms, or both, to encourage a mushrooming of these programs across the country over the last decade. Regardless of the reason, because of the explosive increase in at-risk student programs we are now constantly, almost daily, gaining knowledge about what structures and practices may encourage success and what may not. In Chapter 16 we will look at three specific programmatic recommendations: Positive Youth Development, Educating for Human Greatness, and the NAREN Nine Facets of Quality At-Risk Education.

Before we get to those, carefully read through these general considerations.

- *It is not what, but how, that makes the difference.* Subject matter takes a back seat to a nonpunitive, more positive, individualized, and compassionate means by which it is delivered.
- *Small is better.* Smaller student-to-teacher ratios provide more quality time in which personalization can replace anomie, communication can supplant silence and retreating behaviors, and attitude adjustments become probable. Subject matter and learning methods can be tailored to unique student needs and learning styles.
- *Learn as I do, not as I say.* A startling discovery is that most at-risk students are whole-to-part learners—85 percent, according

to Jerry Conrath. Traditional schools are set up for *part-to-whole* learning: learn this little piece, then this one, then this one, and one day you'll get the "big picture." This is unintelligible, boring, and/or crazy-making for at-risk learners. Research shows that at-risk programs that are experientially and project-based succeed because the bits and pieces that need to be learned fit meaningfully into the big picture (i.e., "Oh, I see a good reason for doing all the work it will take to learn this").

- *I get to choose?* Learning healthy independence includes making choices and enjoying (or paying) the consequences. In a smaller, more closely supervised environment, failures can become the grist for quickly learning effective choice-making "while the iron is still hot."

- *Tough love.* Pullout at-risk programs allow the creation of an extraordinary environment—structured differently, but nevertheless *structured* with a lot of positive attention to student capability and success. Accountability and restitution are major concepts in at-risk education.

- *Clear procedures provide clarity.* What is the mission of the program, its goals? Is it a disciplinary program (a soft jail), or a problem-solving program (therapy)? What are the entrance requirements and exact procedures for getting into the program? What is the structure of both the content and discipline program? How does the program interrelate with the traditional school, the student's family, legal and social services, and the community? All of this and more should be clearly spelled out at the beginning. Of course, a lot will be modified over time as a result of learning from mistakes (and successes), as well as tailored, monitored, and adjusted.

- *Charismatic teachers.* It takes a palm tree to successfully teach in an at-risk program. The teacher has to know how to flex to the ground while having a spine of bamboo. In other words, the teacher who wishes to teach resiliency must model it. A good rule is the 4F Rule: Firm, Fair, Flexible, and Friendly.

- *Charming environments.* The at-risk school or classroom setting should reflect the personality of the humans in it. This becomes a living affirmation to students that their very presence makes a noticeable impact. An at-risk learning environment may not make the feature page of *Better Homes and Gardens,* but it will make the people in it feel like they *belong.*

- *Learn life skills.* Whole-to-part learners want to learn about work, money, family, and activities, with relevant content areas fitted in as needed. Math makes sense when dealing with a real money issue. Writing has meaning when filling out a job application and creating a resume. Honing communication skills is relevant when it can be immediately applied in order to create a more productive or happy relationship.
- *Earlier intervention.* Communities are quite aware that at-risk environments create at-risk youth, and high school is often too-little-too-late for successful intervention to occur. Schools are experimenting with earlier intervention programs that focus on life skills development along with some character building, and in a holistic environment. One possible model, which can be viewed in Appendix III, is the 4R Curriculum: Respectful, Responsible, Reflective, and Resourceful.

A Tongue-in-Cheek Look at What *Not* to Do!

There are many ways to make a point. In such a serious business as at-risk education, perhaps a bit of dark humor is permissible.

Checklist for Program Failure
or
How to Increase the Odds of Your At-Risk Program Failing!

- Make sure it's seen and used as a "dumping ground."
- Insure the curriculum is irrelevant to the real world of its students.
- Dehumanize and sterilize it with a lot of imposed policies, rules, and regulations.
- Hire drill sergeants and burnouts as teachers.
- Underfeed (underfund) it.
- Be vague about the program's purpose and structure.
- Keep the program a secret.
- Overcrowd it.

Checklist for Staffing Failure
or
How to Increase the Odds of Failure by Hiring Educators with the Worst Possible Characteristics!

- Teach the same content in the same way that it is taught in the mainstream; that is, in the identical manner that the student had trouble with the first time!

- Be apathetic, uncaring, and insensitive.
- Exhibit a negative disposition verbally and with body language.
- Teach meaningless and unrelated content to the student.
- Utilize sarcasm and put-downs.
- Be inconsistent, nervous, flighty, and flakey.
- Embarrass students in front of others as a coercive technique.
- Be inflexible.
- Have no sense of humor.
- Treat the students as damaged goods.

At-Risk Students as Objects of Prejudice

It is my firm conviction that there is a deep and abiding prejudice against at-risk students. I mean a prejudice that is no different from the prejudice towards African Americans that, in 1954, made *Brown v. Topeka Board of Education* a necessary decision. This prejudice springs from the same contaminated fountain that pays women less than men for doing the same jobs, calls Asians "gooks" and Mexicans "beaners," and says that certain people, because of their characteristics, do not have the same rights as others. We look down on children whose parents are on welfare, are in prison, or who immigrated to this country and need special help in our schools. In schools today, we still do not unconditionally open our arms to all. We do not.

I think it is a psychological problem. It is a problem that will be very difficult to legislate away, because it rests in the psyche of many in our population. The only way to overcome this prejudice is with exposure to others different from us, in order to discover they are not different at all. Because that is the cause: Fear. Fear of the unknown. Fear that someone will get an unfair share. Fear of what is different. Perhaps legislation can assist with that—mandating that we must associate with those we would prefer not to. If not for forced busing and mandated desegregation, would African Americans have the amount of equal rights that they do have today? Were it not for mandated equal spending on women's sports would we have the female athletic teams (volleyball, basketball and so forth) that we have today?

In the final analysis, however, it will be up to each individual to have the humility to admit that he or she was initially prejudiced and that the reason for that prejudice was a myth clung to in ignorance. It takes a big throat to swallow that pill. How many people have what it takes to do this? And how long before we see differences as spice, and diversity in people as a positive aspect of life? Because that is what diversity really is—variety, enrichment, enhancement, spice.

Anecdotal stories can be misleading, but this next one has stuck with me so strongly for so many years that I believe it to be an iconic example worthy of relating, because it shows a different form of prejudice towards those at risk.

An Anecdote

While teaching my college psychology classes, I hated to just lecture because it seemed a perfect way to take exciting material about our own humanity and turn it into a train to Snoozeville. To combat this malady, one that besets many a college class, I set up a role-playing exercise on decision-making wherein students were sorted into groups of six. Each group played the part of a hospital board in a small town faced with a terrible dilemma. There was one life-saving machine available, and 10 people who needed it within 60 minutes. In other words, nine people were going to die, and one fortunate person was going to live, depending on what the board decided in the next hour. Each role-playing group was given a short biography of all 10 potential recipients.

I knew it was a tough assignment. It almost seemed cruel to put people into such a pressure cooker situation. I relished it. No one fell asleep, and discussions were heated and anxious. Some amazing statements were overheard. Some were compassionate, some quite intelligent, and some shocking. One stood out to me more than others. One of the 10 fake case studies included a young 22-year-old man who had been a high school dropout and was now working in a lumberyard. I heard perky 20-year-old Dixie, with big blue eyes, declare in her group, "Well, the dropout is out. He had his chance and blew it!" Some of her classmates paused, but most just crossed his name off their lists without hesitation.

Having been an at-risk kid who considered dropping out, and having had friends who were forced to dropout because of family issues or were pushed out by a school that would not fit academics to conditions in the kid's life that he could not control, I was horrified at how automatically the word *dropout* made you a social reject.

Did I mention that all of the students in my class were in the teacher education program?

I was so disturbed by her comment that I asked Dixie to stay after class. I liked her. She was a fireball, a dedicated student with a burning desire to be a great teacher.

I said, "Dixie, I overheard your comment about the dropout quickly going into the ineligible category without further consideration."

She repeated, "Yep. He had his chance and blew it."

"Yes, I heard that too. Perhaps there were extenuating circumstances. Maybe he didn't want to drop out, but had to."

"Look, Dr. Jones," she continued, "I studied hard in school—it wasn't easy for me. I have a math phobia and failed it twice here in college, but I got a tutor and passed it. I only got a C, but I passed it, and I never quit. I have little sympathy for kids who quit. They will never amount to anything."

"Who told you that?" I challenged.

"Everybody knows it," she replied, her blue eyes flashing righteously.

Everybody knows it? Well, maybe they know wrong. The dark side is that if enough educators believe they know this, they can make it come true—that way, they won't have to appear wrong. Teachers, more than anyone, often have a thing about being wrong. I should know. I am one. I still remember a student saying to me, "Why do you ask so many questions? Aren't you supposed to know the answers? You're the teacher!"

Funny perhaps, but we just might take it more seriously than even we know. We may subconsciously need to make the self-fulfilling prophecy be fulfilled. Does society need scapegoats to feel better? Why are we so sure that mainstream achievers are worth more to our world than those who don't always fit in? I think it is time to question a lot of things.

This is a good time to look more deeply at the central issue of *respect*. It is a central piece in prejudice, and one that can increase the certainty of success in an educational program for Shadow Children. If at-risk children are to succeed in school they must be respected. Once respect goes out the window, so does any chance for a fruitful relationship between student and teacher. Why would Shadow Children, already downtrodden in so many ways, invest genuine effort in academics unless they feel their educators care for them, respect them, and are willing and able to provide the support they need to help them reclaim themselves?

CHAPTER 15

Angels and Warriors

Educators Who Succeed with Shadow Children

SOMEDAY educators (and hopefully, communities) will look back in shame at how our schools turned its back on today's at-risk children. A school that should offer well-prepared at-risk teachers often places freshmen faculty or burnouts into these teaching positions. Kids should be able to count on having highly trained and skilled educators with the resources necessary to provide the compensatory programs they need. The system should have the ability to launch prevention and intervention programs that at-risk youth desperately need—and need a great deal more than other children.

> None of these children asked to be placed at risk.—Jerry Conrath, teacher and author *Early Prevention*

If our school system insists on revictimizing our youth by officially neglecting them, what message does this send to our children? Today's youth need champions more than ever, and educators are in the perfect position to fill that role—but they need the resources and professional development to do so. Most teachers, myself included, were trained to teach math, or science, or history. We were not trained to teach children—and we were certainly unprepared to teach at-risk children.

Children are the best investment one can make with their tax dollars. In Chapter 2 we saw the costs for not addressing this problem in U.S. schools, which is the school system I am most familiar with. It comes to over $94,000,000,000 *annually*. Or, based on President Obama's broader formula (described in the Preface) $319,000,000,000 annually.

And that figure does nothing but get larger each year. Indeed, in many ways, our children are undoubtedly the best investment possible. From the affectionate vantage point of "our precious children" to the businesslike, multi-billion-dollar annual price tag, or both, it is in our best interest to provide them with the best teachers possible.

The Aspen Institute's Commission on No Child Left Behind (2009) determined that teacher effectiveness is the key ingredient in student success. They also revealed that proper course work or a degree or certification does not necessarily make for the most effective teacher. What accurately measures effectiveness is student progress—the more students who progress under a teacher's supervision, the more effective the teacher. Content is not king, *competence* is.

There is currently a large question in front of public education: What is success? What type of student progress is essential for a teacher to be known as a "good" teacher? If we cannot answer these questions we are left with standardized test scores as the only consistent measure of a teacher. And, if that is what we focus on, it creates another set of problems for education. Namely, if we know that all children are different and believe in diversity as a source of enrichment, but only measure by standardized achievement test scores, we have set ourselves up. It is impossible to standardize students!

How do you measure the effectiveness of teachers who are working with students in these non-standardized content areas?

- Art
- Business
- Drama
- Driver education
- Foreign language
- Health and fitness
- Home and family
- Honors courses
- Independent studies
- Music
- Physical education
- Social studies
- Special education
- Speech
- Sports
- Vocational areas

Add to the above list any kind of new programs or content and, of course, alternative education or pull-out programs for either (1) those who have fallen behind and are in need of compensatory programs to "catch-up," and/or (2) alternative education for the gifted and talented.

What We Focus on Expands

Common sense tells us that what we focus on expands. If you want to feel tired, just keep telling yourself and all around you just how tired you are. If you want to enlarge the negative aspects of anyone or anything, start a list of deficits and shortcomings and keep adding to it. More and more will come to mind. If you wish to feel truly impoverished keep talking and thinking about how broke you are and how unfortunate you are and how crappy your life is and how little you have. (Pretty soon even the national debt will look good to you.)

If we focus on standardized testing as *the* measure of a "good education" it will become all that we see as important and it will grow huge in our eyes, limiting our vision of all the other aspects of what schools and learning can be for students. The things that are memorable about school are rarely the results of a standardized test. Yet there are schools right now spending 2 to 4 weeks of the school year prepping for achievement tests, and that amount of time is expanding. Yet no one agrees on what a "good education" is. What is important for a student to know? What—learned now—will serve a student's future well? Who is the "best" teacher?

Without answers to these questions, why are we spending so much time trying to standardize our students? With this focus, diversity will become our enemy. Tension and competition among teachers, administrators, and schools (and states) will mount to a fever pitch. Collaboration, creativity, team-teaching, and flexibility will become concepts to avoid.

Focusing on Teaching

NAREN research shows that what makes for effectiveness in at-risk education comes in two categories that we liberally, deliberately, and dramatically label Angel Educators and/or Warrior Educators. Both categories of educators have several things in common. They prize learning and student progress. They see education as having the power to change life for the better and they see themselves as having high self-efficacy as instruments of betterment for kids. These and a few other commonalities are internal attributes, and usually invisible. What is amazing is how the external attributes of these educators can appear to mirror the opposite of who they really are. It is the visible means by which these educators relate to at-risk learners, in particular, that is noticeably dramatic. Most highly successful at-risk educators are either Angel Educators or Warrior Educators. These labels have nothing to do with religion or with violence. Rather, they help to understand, underline, define, and explain.

The quotes below are from a survey of over 90 at-risk students in alternative programs, and 110-plus current teachers who were formerly at-risk students.

Angel Educators

Angel educators are teachers who, despite being quiet, low key, and studious, are remarkably successful with at-risk students.

- *Compassionate.* This is number one for a reason. Angel teachers may be no more compassionate than Warrior teachers, but they show it clearly. It is quite obvious they *care* about children. They seem to look past symptomatic behaviors of defiance, gruffness, resistance, and reluctance sometimes shown by at-risk kids, and, as one student said, can "peer into my soul with eyes of concern."
- *Present.* Being present is obvious to children. "She wanted to be with us!" People who do not want to work with an at-risk kid are either bitter because they are required to be working with this child, or they are distant and focused on something other than the child in the moment, meaning they would rather be someplace else.
- *A Light Being.* This difficult to define, but one participant said it best: "It seemed like her feet never touched the floor. I used to watch to make sure because rumor had it that she was an angel and might be able to fly." Light beings seem to be quiet, soft, and almost spooky in their silence, suddenly showing up at your elbow when you need help. "Ms._____ scared the hell out of me, as she seemed to materialize just behind my shoulder when I was having trouble!"
- *Gentle.* "She never raised her voice the whole year!" Angel educators are not always teachers. A principal may be the most

powerful educator in the whole building. "Mr. C always called us by name, and never yelled at us." "Our principal was a great guy. He never yelled at us, would smile softly at us and knew all our names. I never figured out how he knew everyone's name. I realized years later that maybe he only knew my name!" Most seasoned educators know that you do not force anything onto people. You nudge them gently in a direction until it is their idea. Shouting, or being angry, just causes fear and resistance. Most at-risk kids have already experienced enough force to last a lifetime.

- *Focused on Positivism.* "She never criticized us!" "Mr. H only marked the correct answers on our tests, not the wrong ones. He always said, 'Let's build on our strengths, people!'" Great teachers know that everyone loves to talk about their good points, and withdraw or get defensive when you focus on their negative points. It has never dawned on some teachers that what you focus on expands. Once a teacher understands this fact, things go better for them because they see the room begin to fill up with a pleasant, positive, and progressive atmosphere.

Warrior Educators

Warrior Educators may appear loud and gruff, but they have hearts of gold. Warrior Educators exhibit their lives on their sleeves. They often have troubled backgrounds and have learned from the school of hard knocks. Now they want to help at-risk kids get the break perhaps they never had. They want to be the teachers they never had, but so desperately needed.

Perhaps the Warrior Educator is teaching—though they act more like a professional wrestler—because they were inspired by a teacher or person who changed their life. But beneath their bark is a caring, loving person dedicated to at-risk youth.

- *Tough.* Battle-scarred, perhaps, or maybe protecting themselves from being too vulnerable, the Warrior Educator's gruffness is apparent, but not meant to harm anyone. They are often surprised when told they appear aggressive or loud, but they will not deny they are intense. "Mrs. N____ acted like there was no tomorrow and tenaciously moved us along like a freight train on an emergency mission!"

- *Street Savvy.* When in a dark and dangerous place, this is the person you would want with you: smart, capable of handling the unknown, and fearless. "My best teachers at the Tech School had all been scarred by life!" To which one of my students added: "And some had done a little scarring themselves. My history teacher was a Vietnam vet and said he never felt more alive than when there, but he wouldn't talk about things he had done there. 'Let sleeping dogs lie' was one of his expressions. But he taught like we were lucky to have this chance to learn. 'The things people take for granted in the United States do not apply everywhere. It is a privilege to have people care enough about you to teach you—and you *will* learn!' he would say with a smile—but he meant it!"

- *Goal Focused.* Whereas Angel Educators may appear more needs-based—meaning they deal with each child in a nurse-like manner—Warrior Educators appear more focused on outcomes. "He would start off by saying, 'Today we WILL accomplish the following things!' then he would proceed to do exactly that, repeating it at the end of the class with, 'Look what you did!' That was powerful to me. Every day I could see what I had gained. Other classes seemed to slip by with me being unchanged, but Mr. W_____ made it look like we had just gone up a step on the universal stairwell, and would never be the same."

- *Overcomes Obstacles.* Warrior Educators are at war. They may even use warlike words, such as "conquering," "winning the battle," or "victory." Angel Educators seem to look on the bright side whereas Warrior Educators see the world as a challenge, or a race against an imaginary clock with dire consequences if one loses. They believe in the power of effort and make it clear that, not unlike a mountain climber, if you try hard enough you can make it. "Mrs. C____ never gave up on us, and said we could 'win the race of life' if we just wanted it bad enough and were determined enough."

Conclusion

Does this mean that only a clearly defined Angel or Warrior Educator can be successful with at-risk children? Of course not! Many educators are a combination of the two. What I have attempted to do here is make it clear what works, and show that great teachers can be quite different in their effectiveness and approaches to learning and students. On the other hand, a very successful educator once said to me, "The secret to a great program is not *what* you teach but who teaches it." When I asked him to clarify he said, "Real learning is about relationships—with either the content alone or with a teacher who inspires you to be all you can be. A good teacher makes learning enjoyable or meaningful, but a great teacher makes learning seem essential as well."

Mentioned in this chapter are some factors common to successful at-risk educators. Every effective teacher usually also possesses a sense of humor and great enthusiasm for the academic content or learning processes. Humor and enthusiasm appear as significant labels applied to most educators who are seen as exceptional by their former students. Educators of at-risk children are this and more: They are Angels and Warriors who do not know the word *quit*. They fight failure as if it were a dragon, as it may well be. Above all else, they care deeply about their children's futures and are not afraid to show it.

You are fortunate if you have had one of these educators in your life. There is no reason we could not attract and train more of them, but the field of education is timid it seems—unwilling to get into the character education of teachers, although it would impact the character education of students directly. We just need to think a bit and then be willing to announce these findings, and in our teacher training aim directly at the target of creating Angel and Warrior Educators with deliberate and determined enthusiasm. It can be done. I have seen it happen.

CHAPTER 16

A Case for Separate At-Risk Education Standards

Programs That Work

THERE is little consistency in applying quality standards to educational programs for at-risk students. Yet, if we take the preceding chapters to heart, it is obvious that we must care for Shadow Children enough to shape the educational environment for an optimal fit to their unique needs. Since its inception on January 1, 2001, NAREN has been attempting to derive from all available research a means by which quality at-risk programs could be instituted systemically and nationwide. This has taken the form of creating a vehicle that directs resources to more effectively stem this tide of discouraged learners.

What follows is a general introduction to the NAREN schema for evaluating at-risk educational programs. It is also a succinct attempt to provide guidance and leadership to establish a foundation for effective design and implementation of a quality program for at-risk education. Assessment is often the Trojan horse of educational reform.

Three Models That Work

The NAREN Nine. Positive Youth Development. Educating for Human Greatness. I have chosen these three exemplary models because I know they work. There are obviously other models that work. NAREN associates have access to a private database of over 100 programs that have worked with at-risk youth in a school setting.

The three models presented here are different and powerful approaches to providing quality programming for at-risk youth. Pushing more of the same mainstream curriculum they have struggled with or have not been able to succeed with seems silly, but it is done over and over again in school systems across the United States. Many alternative programs in one state just stick at-risk kids in a bare room with Blue Books (the mainstream curriculum in a cookbook/workbook format) for half a day, then put them in work study the other half—and pretty much write them off. One day we will look back and realize what we did to these kids. We will be horrified how we revictimized these victims: talked down to them, treated them as second class (or lower) citizens, and, worst of all, showed quite obviously that we held little hope for them to amount to anything. If we were that good at predicting the future we would be at the racetrack! How dare we imperiously look down our noses at these kids, not really knowing them at all, just because the pre-ordained curriculum—one that does not acknowledge their uniquity—is not befitting them. All three models of these models are high on personalization. The key word to remember is *relationship*.

The NAREN Nine

NAREN titles its research-based scaffolding *Quality Facets of At-Risk Education Programs*. It currently comes in the form of a 130-page Self-Study Kit that allows schools to either build new effective programs from scratch, revitalize programs that are not working, or evaluate existing programs.

There are three major themes residing within each facet of the NAREN Nine:

- *Curriculum wrapping:* personalizing the curriculum in a holistic manner that acknowledges the value of each student's individuality
- *Authentic assessment:* clear indicators that a student and staff are moving in successful directions
- *Monitoring and adjusting:* humility to admit mistakes, along with subsequent willingness to redirect efforts in more productive directions.

Quality Facets of At-Risk Education Programs

The nine facets for quality at-risk programs that NAREN staff and researchers have identified as effective are listed below. Experience has shown that there is a high correlation between the number of facets adhered to and the program's success. Success is defined as overcoming obstacles that previously blocked the student from learning and completing the program. (Usually a high school diploma is the capstone experience.)

Accelerated Academic Curriculum

Most at-risk students learn differently and not at all slowly when they are engaged appropriately to their learning styles and needs. High expectations that are reasonable and reachable are called for along with an integration of academic and work-based learning. *Meaning* is a key component to learning, and especially for at-risk learners. Acceleration is accomplished by setting high and clear goals with meaningful material matched to learning style—signifying that each student has his/her learning individually prescribed.

Strong Literacy Component

"Can't read? Go to jail!" might as well be the banner over the swelling population that is entering our jails and prisons. Next to alcohol and other drug abuse (AODA) issues, illiteracy is the number one qualifier for poverty and/or criminal behavior. The logical and rightful place to stem this tide is in the school. All academic achievement rests solidly on the ability to read and comprehend well. NAREN certification would mean that a program is (1) assessing reading and comprehension upon entry into the program, (2) prescribing appropriate literacy activities, and (3) monitoring and adjusting the literacy curriculum for each student commensurate with individual needs and abilities in order to ensure success. Note: A twenty-first century addition to the traditional definition of "being able to read and write" is computer literacy. The computer has become an essential part of our ability to communicate effectively with the world and each another.

Deliberate Self-Management Program

NAREN research reveals that if an at-risk program is to be effective it must include a deliberate atmosphere and program of social skills in self-management and responsibility. School personnel must work toward objectives that increase student self-control, school success, attachment and commitment to education, self-efficacy expectations, and belief in a structure (e.g., guidelines or rules). In schools where such a program is well implemented, student conduct improves substantially.

Personalized Curriculum

NAREN research reveals that in order for an at-risk curriculum to be effective it must shape itself to the student. NAREN strongly encourages deliberate *curriculum wrapping* as an intervention procedure with a curricular foundation. Each student has different individual needs and problems as well as a personal life journey. A personalized curriculum holistically recognizes that one cannot separate academics from personal issues, and it is structured to deliberately and definitively address issues interfering with achievement and success in all facets of a student's life.

Project-Experiential-Work Orientation

NAREN research reveals that if an at-risk curriculum is to be effective it must offer a whole-to-part curriculum—students fully engaged in a productive enterprise that makes learning relevant to their learning style. A solid work component with major emphasis on developing a positive and productive work ethic is essential to high school age at-risk students. School-based businesses run by students are highly encouraged. For elementary school level at-risk students this component is still important, but experiences should be age-appropriate, such as a mock store where students can learn about working in groups, handling money, planning, decision making, prioritizing, problem solving, and accountability.

Smaller School and Class Size

Research does not conclusively show a *direct* correlation between smaller class size and increases in achievement scores. NAREN believes that success is not only about content-centered scores but also about self-esteem, confidence, and the ability to be productive and healthy. A key factor in this kind of success with at-risk youth is often creation of closer student-teacher and student-student relationships. Smaller classes allow teachers to individually prescribe instruction, monitor progress, and encourage more interactivity. Smaller schools foster a sense of family/community, identity building, and caring relationships that enable successful adjustments and transitions.

Solid Planning and Administrative Support System

NAREN research reveals that if an at-risk curriculum is to be effective it must have a clear mission statement based on a definitively stated philosophy of education, and commensurately cohesive teaching and learning strategies that are based on research and theory. A collaborative, communicative, and supportive administration model is highly recommended, one that makes it quite evident that staff and students are both highly prized. The main ingredient of support is insuring that resources needed for optimal learning are provided. Education benefits us all but its main goal is for the edification of the children. Resources should go for this goal before they go for anything else, and it is the sum total of the administration's job description to provide those resources in support of the teaching-learning paradigm.

Collaborative Community Model

NAREN research reveals that if an at-risk program is to be effective it must involve collaborative efforts with various educational stakeholders in the community: parents, business leaders, law enforcement and the judicial system, social service agencies, and institutions of religious faith. Evaluations of community involvement programs indicate that these programs can consistently affect positive outcomes for attendance and persistence in school. The effects range from small to substantial but are always positive. Not to be ignored is the positive influence of local higher education institutions. They are often influential with students prior to high school graduation in numerous ways and set a tone of expectation regarding life-long learning as a viable option for all.

Comprehensive Staff Development Program

Some alternative programs come and go with few lasting benefits for their students, and teachers often become suspicious and reluctant to buy into further "promising" reform efforts. Alternative at-risk models are very complex and often require intensive study, effort, and time to effectively implement. A successful program must include a deliberate and pertinent staff development schema in which teachers are in contact with skilled trainers in a variety of professional development settings at the school and in the classroom. Distance and online learning, in-house interactive involvement with experts, video conferencing, attendance at conferences and trainings, and professional association memberships, all sitting squarely on a needs-based curriculum, offer substantial assistance and support for modern teachers in an educational world.

Conclusion to the NAREN Nine

Certification, standards, guidelines, code points, rubrics—what are they all about? They are concerned with establishing a structure, or scaffolding, that channels resources (time, money, energy, people, materials, etc.) in the most productive of directions. It is always a matter of opinion(s), but research-based opinion is less speculative and has been field-tested under controlled circumstances in an attempt to sort out the variables that truly make a substantial difference toward improving the chances of success for at-risk youth.

Professional dialogue is needed. It is apparent that earnest educators rarely have enough opportunity, even locally, to participate in meaningful discussions with each other about the school and its key purpose—teaching and learning. A popular component of the NAREN Nine certification process is the dialogue(s) over pedagogical issues that occur among the staff as they undergo the documentation and assessment of their program(s).

Positive Youth Development

With permission from the American Psychological Association (APA), I have taken the liberty to distill an additional and potentially powerful proactive assessment model from an exceptionally well-researched APA article by Richard F. Catalano and others (2002), *Positive Youth Development in the United States: Research Findings on Evaluations of Positive Youth Development Programs.* This research-based report not only delineates, but also clearly defines, 15 characteristics of effective programming for youth.

1. Promotes bonding
2. Fosters resilience
3. Promotes social competence
4. Promotes emotional competence

5. Promotes cognitive competence
6. Promotes behavioral competence
7. Promotes moral competence
8. Fosters self-determination
9. Fosters spirituality
10. Fosters self-efficacy
11. Fosters clear and positive identity
12. Fosters belief in the future
13. Provides recognition for positive behavior
14. Provides opportunities for prosocial involvement
15. Fosters prosocial norms

Positive Youth Development Characteristics Defined

- *Bonding program facet:* One or more of the program's components focuses on developing the child's emotional attachment and commitment to a healthy adult, positive peers, school, community, or culture.
- *Resilience program facet:* Program emphasizes healthy strategies for adaptive coping responses to change and stress, and promotes psychological flexibility and a capacity toward successful outcomes.
- *Social competence program facet:* Program provides training in developmentally appropriate interpersonal skills that help youth integrate feelings, thinking, and actions in order to achieve specific social and interpersonal goals, and rehearsal strategies for practicing these skills. These skills included communication, assertiveness, refusal and resistance, conflict resolution, and interpersonal negotiation strategies for use with peers and adults.
- *Emotional competence program facet:* Program develops the skills of youth for identifying feelings in self or others, skills for managing emotional reactions or impulses, or skills for building the youth's self-management strategies, empathy, self-soothing, or frustration tolerance.
- *Cognitive competence program facet:* Program seeks to influence a child's cognitive abilities, processes, or outcomes, including academic performance, logical and analytic thinking, problem solving, decision making, planning, goal setting, and self-talk skills.

- *Behavioral competence program facet:* Program teaches skills and provides reinforcement for effective behavior choices and action patterns, including nonverbal and verbal strategies.
- *Moral competence program facet:* Program seeks to promote empathy, respect for cultural or societal rules and standards, a sense of right and wrong, or a sense of moral or social justice.
- *Self-determination program facet:* Program seeks to increase youths' capacity for empowerment, autonomy, independent thinking, or self-advocacy; their ability to live and grow by self-determined internal standards and values (may or may not include group values).
- *Spirituality program facet:* Program promotes the development of beliefs in a higher power, internal reflection or meditation, or supports youth in exploring a spiritual belief system or sense of spiritual identity, meaning, or practice.
- *Self-efficacy program facet:* Program includes personal goal setting, coping and mastery skills, or techniques to change self-defeating cognitions and negative self-efficacy expectancies (the perception that one can achieve desired goals through one's own action).
- *Clear and positive identity program facet:* Program seeks to develop healthy identity formation and achievement in youth, including positive identification with a social or cultural subgroup that supports their healthy development of a sense of self.
- *Belief in the future program facet:* Program seeks to influence a child's belief in his/her future potential, goals, options, choices, or long-range hopes and plans, or promotes youth's optimism about a healthy and productive adult life.
- *Recognition for positive behavior program facet:* Program creates response systems for rewarding, recognizing, or reinforcing children's prosocial behaviors.
- *Opportunities for prosocial involvement program facet:* Program offers activities and events in which youths can actively participate, make a positive contribution, and experience positive social exchanges.
- *Fosters social norms program facet:* Program employs strategies for encouraging youths to develop clear and explicit standards for behaviors that minimize health risks and support prosocial involvement.

Conclusion to Positive Youth Development

With some expertise and effort, the 15 characteristics of Positive Youth Development could be productively modified into an effective assessment instrument for at-risk education programs. Much like the NAREN Nine, each of the characteristics above could be converted into a standard statement, along with indicators for each standard, some of which are alluded to in these descriptions. Those indicators would then be broken out into benchmarks and rubrics for accurate rating of program components.

Educating for Human Greatness

Lynn Stoddard spent over 50 of his years as a teacher, then a principal. After a few decades of observing education he began to wonder why education continued to focus on what is wrong with kids. In his experience there was a lot that is right with kids. He felt that if the focus was shifted to the good things in children, the talents and inclinations they naturally had, the classroom would be a lot more productive.

Lynn Stoddard begs the question: Whatever killed the natural Need to Know, and must it remain a permanent death? Cannot the thing we call education be a place where we restore learning to its natural state of being, fascinated with growing in our knowing?

Lynn Stoddard suggests that we pause and imagine what a school would be like if kids were all fascinated with learning. (Wouldn't that be wonderful?) A school like that would probably have few, if any, discipline problems. Absenteeism numbers would shrink and there would be a notable reduction in dropout figures. Certainly a school like that would not be filled with bored students and frazzled teachers trying to figure out how to entice students to learn something they do not want to learn.

Using simple and natural concepts, Mr. Stoddard and the teachers in his school began eliminating the many high pressure, punitive, and behaviorist practices that were forcing more and more memorization upon children just to drive up test scores. They eventually instituted a plan to realign their school to recapture that natural learning zone found inside each child, and after several years of field-testing named it Educating for Human Greatness.

His model is briefly described below. It is included here as it deliberately countermands the deficiency model we live with in many of our schools today. It is a start and needs more field testing, but Stoddard sees it as a new paradigm and a unifying model for reinventing education. He sees the major purpose of schools to be the following: Develop great human beings to be contributors to society. He sees this happening by facilitating growth in these seven powers/dimensions:

1. *Identity:* The power of self-worth derived from developing one's unique talents and gifts
2. *Inquiry:* The power of curiosity and efficient, effective investigation
3. *Interaction:* The powers of love, human relationships, communication, and cooperation
4. *Initiative:* The power of self-discipline and intrinsic motivation
5. *Imagination:* The power of creativity in its many forms, including innovative problem-solving and using. Use all of the arts to nurture all forms of imagination and creativity
6. *Intuition:* The power of the heart to sense truth and develop emotional intelligence
7. *Integrity:* The power of honesty and responsibility

The Big Ideas

- Nurture the development of *positive human diversity.* Help students develop as unique individuals with their own sets of talents, gifts, interests, and abilities. Cease trying to standardize and make students alike in knowledge and skills. It is not only impossible, but it is detrimental to the whole system, including administrators, students, teachers, and parents.
- Teach reading, writing, math, and thousands of other disciplines as tools of inquiry, interaction, avenues to talent and gift development, and all seven dimensions of human greatness. Cease teaching skills and subjects as isolated ends in and of themselves. If you wish to develop voracious readers, for example, focus on creating an insatiable curiosity for topics that interest the student. Basic skills and all knowledge are learned much better as a process of inquiry and with intrinsic motivation, rather than by extrinsic imposition.
- Shift from useless standardized testing to authentic accountability and assessment of growth in the seven powers of greatness.

The Role of Teachers (Including Parents)

The basic act of teaching is to organize and provide experiences that stimulate inquiry, imagination, respectful interaction, and the other powers of greatness. A teacher, looking through eyes of affirmation and appreciation, should see the unlimited special potential of each child. For more details visit the Educating for Human Greatness website (www.educatingforhumangreatness.com).

The Six Pivotal Principles

The principle planks in current education platform are quite vague. Depending on who you speak with, they may vary quite a bit. Stoddard felt we needed to be clear about our guidance system of principles if we are to make progress. Following are the Six Pivotal Principles upon which the platform of Educating for Human Greatness depends. One should probably read Lynn Stoddard's book, *Educating for Human Greatness,* to grasp the importance of these six principles. But the first principle immediately and dramatically separates Educating for Human Greatness from current public school practices.

- *Principle 1—Value Positive Human Diversity:* This is the foundation principle upon which the other principles are built. For many years the mission of public education has been that of standardizing students, of diligently trying to make children alike in knowledge and skills. Educating for Human Greatness takes the opposite approach: nurturing each child as a special person to develop their unique gifts, talents, abilities, and skills that can be developed to benefit society.
- *Principle 2—Draw Forth Potential:* This principle recognizes that each child is unique, with a unique set of gifts and talents. These special assets can only be accessed through a process of loving interaction. It is a process of bringing out the best that is in each person. *Drawing forth* is the opposite of trying to fill students with information. It requires an entirely different set of skills. In contrast to traditional education, which focuses on helping children overcome deficits, this principle works on helping children to build on their unique assets.
- *Principle 3—Respect Autonomy:* In the traditional system students

are not encouraged to be responsible for their own education. This principle recognizes that, regardless of what others do or say, each person ultimately decides for themselves what information or influences he/she will use for growth. I invite readers to respect the inalienable right of every person to be responsible for his or her own learning and behavior. When learners are freed from coercion and given responsibility for their own learning, amazing things happen.

- *Principle 4—Invite Inquiry:* Educating for Human Greatness expands the difference between the imposed, compulsory learning of today's schools—and education that is the result of personal inquiry. The first is shallow and temporary. The second is deep and enduring. When a synthetic, packaged curriculum is imposed on teachers to impose on their students, it often squelches personal inquiry. On the other hand, pursuing personal interests invites students to ask questions and seek knowledge and wisdom.

- *Principle 5—Support Professionalism:* Teachers in public education are told what to teach and, often, how to teach. In Educating for Human Greatness, teachers are no longer treated as workers on an educational assembly line, but as creative professionals who know how to diagnose the needs of each child, work with parents, and nurture positive diversity. With this view, teaching becomes a true profession and a delicate art; a sensitive, creative endeavor that responds to the special, striving needs of each child.

- *Principle 6—CommUNITY for Great Schools:* Parents and teachers need to become full partners to help children grow in greatness. The traditional role of parents as spectators on the educational sidelines can be changed to that of active team partners united with teachers to help children realize their amazing potential as valuable contributors to society.

What follows is a succinct chart showing the differences between conventional education and Educating for Human Greatness. Is this idealism? Most certainly. Does it work? Yes, it has! It is being used today in various schools due to a rebirth of interest in Educating for Human Greatness. Lynn Stoddard's goal is to encourage teachers to begin to use it and provide encouragement for others to do the same. Clearly, more action research is called for.

A Comparison of Two Philosophies of Education

Conventional Education	Educating for Human Greatness
• Student achievement in curriculum (i.e., grade point averages) is the main goal of public education	• Human greatness is the main goal. Parents and teachers unite to help students become valuable contributors to society.
• A common core curriculum, imposed by politicians, is the boss over parents, teachers, and students.	• Curriculum is the servant of parents and teachers, chosen and adapted by them to embrace a variety of needs in all youngsters.
• The aim is for standardization—attempting to make children alike in knowledge and skills. National and state standards for student uniformity are imposed.	• The aim is to nurture human diversity—helping students discover and develop their unique talents and gifts. High standards are adopted for developing student individuality.
• Has a low estimate of human potential. Ranks people with I.Q. tests.	• Sees unlimited potential in every person. Acknowledges that human intelligence is not numerically measurable.
• Tries to measure student growth in curriculum.	• Assesses student growth in the qualities of human greatness and contributive behavior.
• Parents are not meaningfully involved in public or private education.	• Parents are involved as full and equal partners with teachers to help students grow in their qualities of greatness.

Conclusion

The purpose of this chapter has been an answer to the perennial question, "What are we supposed to do with these kids?" In this chapter, three different models utilized in the field have been briefly explained. They clearly show that something *can* be done—there is hope.

This chapter proposes there is more than one way to assess an at-risk program. Why do I say "assess" instead of "build"? Because we are obsessed in the United States right now with assessment via the drive for common standards backed by serious money from the federal government. However, the assessment for this current "reform movement" is in the form of standardized testing. Most savvy educational researchers know that assessment is the Trojan horse of educational reform. If common standards are what you assess, that is what schools will become. There is so much wrong with one-size-fits-all education that these same savvy educational researchers are nearly speechless.

Some believe that we are beyond reform in education, that we need to invent school all over again. We need to bulldoze the school concept of same books, same time, for all kids. We have entered the twenty-first century and need to look like it. Some feel we are doing a great job now of preparing kids to live in the 1950s. Everyone has an opinion on education because we all sat in desks for years and years. We also have a large population of school haters. Right now, if we do *not* intervene with a new, more differentiated form of education, we will raise another generation of school haters—only this generation will be larger.

So look back over the three models presented and think: If we assessed our school by each of these, how different would our school look? Take each model separately and imagine the results if we used the NAREN Nine, the 15 characteristics of Positive Youth Development, or the seven dimensions and six principles of Educating for Human Greatness. What would school look like? How would it impact *all* children in the K–12 system?

Whichever model you might use, the critical factor is that a quality, coherent, and *consistent* framework is utilized to guarantee excellence in educational programming for at-risk youth. If you are improving performances of at-risk kids, imagine what would happen with the mainstream population. It would soar! There would be little need for alternative, special, or separate programs.

Utilizing standardized achievement scoring as the measure of success forces schools into two areas of dilemma: (1) It is impossible to make students alike, and (2) it mandates separation because of this impossibility. I would like to say that standardized testing as the means of measuring success is much ado about nothing, but the truth is that people are being hurt by it. It is cold and deliberate, and misleading us down a thorny path to disaster.

It is important to note that assessment instruments are more than just a way to evaluate how we/they are doing. They are creative and formative as well.

Q: How do we build a great at-risk educational program?

A: Start with the instrument by which you are going to eventually assess it, and build accordingly.

Q: Our program is off the ground, but wobbly. How can we fix it?
A: Get the current pulse and profile of what is going on with the
(eventual) assessment instrument and map out a plan for
modifying the direction of the program accordingly.

Again, no child asked to be placed at risk. No at-risk child knows how to fix their problem(s). They rely on us to help them help themselves and they deserve, just like anyone else in the school system, to be exposed to the best educational programming possible. These are not throwaway human beings; they are children—children looking to adults to show them the way to utilize their intellect effectively to benefit themselves, others, and our society.

Quality programming for at-risk youth is a reassuring way of saying (1) we are professionals who care, (2) you are in the good hands, and (3) you are not alone in your struggle.

NAREN urges educational systems to rapidly adopt a unique and realistic set of at-risk education standards that address the positive diversity in students. This, in order to open doorways to at-risk educational reform, so that all students have an opportunity to attain success.

CHAPTER 17

Prevention and Intervention

Factors Influencing Prevention/Intervention Programming

SHOULD schools be involved in prevention/intervention programs? Let us first look at the population demographics affecting today's youth.

As stated previously, the twenty-first century family has evolved drastically and has a distinctively different impact on its children (Weissberg et al. 2003):

- Divorce rates are now at 50 percent.
- Unmarried women commonly bear and rear children.
- Dual career parents are the norm.
- Only 30 percent of families have a biological parent working at home and the other in a career outside the home.

Although family configurations have significantly changed and family dysfunction has also significantly increased over the last 50 years, schools have not changed commensurately. Drastic changes in the makeup of modern family constellations and the statistically significant increase in abuse and neglect of children call for the school to morph itself into a posture where it is anticipating and meeting the curve of change rather than being constantly behind it.

Q: What is the general mental health of children today?
A: A Surgeon General's report indicates that one of every five children experiences symptoms of a mental disorder during the course of any one year. However, 75–80 percent of these children fail to receive appropriate services (and most still come to school untreated) (U.S. Department of Health and Human Services 2008).

Q: What is the level of risk behaviors in today's youth?
A: Not good.

- 30 percent of 14–17 year-olds engage in multiple high-risk behaviors in any one year.
- Another 35 percent are considered medium risk, being involved with one or two problem behaviors.
- 35 percent have little or no involvement with problem behaviors but still require strong and consistent support to avoid becoming involved (Dryfoos 1997)

Q: What can we truthfully say about the coping skills of today's youth?
A: Relatively low percentages of young people have personal competencies, values, attitudes, and environmental supports that protect against high-risk behavior and encourage the growth of positive behaviors (Benson et al. 1998).

So, the answer to the big question:

Q: Should schools be involved in prevention/intervention programs?
A: It appears that schools are the natural and perhaps only logical choice to launch a widespread, intelligent, organized, and consistent intervention program.

Q: What are the objects of prevention/intervention?
A: NAREN suggests the following hit list of targeted issues that often need to be addressed with prevention/intervention strategies for Shadow Children:

- physical illness
- mental/emotional disorders
- violence
- school failure
- health-damaging risk behaviors
- poverty
- criminal behaviors
- ignorance

Q: What differentiates prevention from intervention?
A: *Prevention* = actions taken to decrease the number of new cases or incidences of a negative outcome. *Intervention* = actions taken to lower the prevalence of existing cases or incidences of a negative outcome.

Prevention

NAREN identifies these four approaches to prevention.

1. *Promotion prevention* is not driven by emphasis on illness or social disease, but by focusing on the enhancement of well-being. Promotion is utilized to build competence and self-esteem and increase the quality of life in a general or specific population.
2. *Universal prevention* targets the general public or a whole population group that has not been identified on the basis of individual risk.
3. *Selective prevention* targets individuals or population subgroups that have been identified as possessing biological, psychological, or social factors that place them at higher than average likelihood of being placed at risk.
4. *Indicated prevention* focuses on high-risk individuals with detectable symptoms or biological, psychological, or social markers that place them at higher than average likelihood of not succeeding in life if intervention does not take place. It is this group that, based on local indicators, is often selected for alternative programs.

Intervention

NAREN acknowledges that there are many interpretations of the intervention concept, varying across theoretical constructs, value structures, target populations, methodologies, timing, and preferred outcomes, but there are eight proven systemic characteristics of successful at-risk intervention programs for Shadow Children. You can measure the success of an intervention program by the number and sincerity of the characteristics below.

1. *Clearly defined target population:* Recipients of an intervention should be clearly identified. A graphic, unreasonable example that illustrates this point: if one could obtain a group photograph of all community members, the target population should be easily identified with an "X" over each member that is to directly benefit from the intervention. This takes time, thought, and discussion.
2. *Clearly defined precipitating behaviors:* The goal of intervention is to halt or reduce negative outcomes. The behaviors that lead to those outcomes are not always clear. Does television lead to more

aggression? Does the lack of a recreation center create gang formation? Can after-school programs reduce teen drug use? It takes time and diligent research to answer these questions.

3. *Comprehensive program approach:* Research into existing successful programs shows over and over again that because human beings are multifaceted, so must effective programs be. Collaboration among the school staff, and between the school, the family, social agencies, law enforcement, local businesses, and religious institutions are needed if the new safety net is to be strong. This means reaching out with an intervention that stays consistent over time.

4. *Clearly defined program goals:* Goals need to be defined with crystal clear objectives and measurable outcomes. Does a 50 percent reduction in underage drinking mean success or failure? If the dropout rate is reduced by three students a year, is it enough to crow about, or does it mean the program has failed? This calls for thought, discussion, and agreement.

5. *Clearly defined indicators/timelines:* Perhaps there is too much emphasis on final outcomes of programs, and equal attention needs to be given to processes, ongoing practices, climate, and social and emotional aspects. How can one tell if a program is succeeding along the way without waiting for the end results?

6. *Appropriately funded:* If you cannot see the budget, don't start the program. Projected costs need to be thoughtfully determined and backed with serious commitment. It is certainly counterproductive—and almost cruel—to begin a program dedicated to betterment and raise hopes only to dash them (again) because the financial resources are inadequate.

7. *Stakeholder ownership:* It is one thing to get others involved. It is yet another to foster ownership in all parties. The old expression, "In for a penny, in for a pound" is relevant. All partners in the collaborative endeavor should have something to gain OR lose by their involvement. Communication is key. (Don't forget that the main recipient of the intervention, the at-risk child, must also buy in!)

8. *Persistence:* Persistence always wins, and half-hearted efforts rarely do when it comes to intervention. All stakeholders must be in it for the long haul—not surprised if it takes years to see results, but pleasantly surprised if it doesn't. It can take as long to solve a

problem as it did to create it. Educational leadership dedicated to a role of constant and long-term support will play a large part in any formula for success.

Selecting for Intervention

Ask a class of 30 kindergartners, "How many of you are going to have a fantastic life?" Every hand will go up. Every face will be shining, smiling, and full of hope and promise. If you come back to these children 12 years later and ask the same question, only 30 percent will raise their hands. That 30 percent are those who are still in school. Why?

Because, if our current statistics remain intact:

- 18 percent of the original group will have dropped out and/or run away
- One will have committed suicide
- One will have been murdered
- One will have died from an alcohol or drug-related incident
- One will be incarcerated

Too often when you attend alternative education or at-risk conferences, the conversations on intervention and the ideas are directed at high school students. Isn't this too late? It is certainly too late for the dead ones. Certainly too late for the incarcerated ones. Certainly too late for those that are so mentally ill from years of dysfunctional family abuse and neglect, meaninglessness, hopelessness, and helplessness that they are now too depressed to absorb much of anything. Too late for the 70 percent who do not raise their hands.

Personally, I am privileged like few others in this field when it comes to the gathering of current educational information. I travel the country speaking at conferences, working with schools, and have spoken with educators all over the United States. In addition, I am a graduate professor of courses with teachers who are in the classroom teaching at-risk students all day long.

Over the years I have listened to thousands of teachers and administrators, hearing their concerns and discussing at-risk education programs, practices, and issues with them. Over and over, some common pieces regarding intervention issues rise to the top of the concern list. Please pay attention to my students, educators in the field from all over the United States, who are speaking through me. They are experienced, insightful, and intelligent professionals who can tell us what works and what roadblocks they have experienced. These roadblocks take the form of quandaries such as:

- Why do they wait until high school to start trying to help these kids?
- We know kids are at risk, but there is no funding/time/personnel.
- There are so many kids who are at risk in our schools that we don't know where to start.
- The issues impacting today's youth are beyond the scope and reach of the teacher or school.
- There are so many personal issues in kids that even if we were trained to deal with these issues, we would not have the time needed to teach content sufficiently enough to do well on the standardized tests that we are being measured against.
- There seems to be no way to identify these kids in advance of trouble, so we wind up being police officers and social workers instead of teachers.

Many of these quandaries are caused, or certainly exacerbated, by difficulty with identification and timing: By what criteria and when do we select the at-risk students for compensatory assistance?

Candidates for Intervention

If you attend conferences and conventions in the genre of at-risk education, alternative education, charter schools, or drop-out prevention, you will notice that almost all attendees are working at the secondary level in education. This is the legacy created by a phrase that we have lived with for so long: "At risk of dropping out of school."

As mentioned in Chapter 5, originally this phrase meant being behind in a certain number of Carnegie units to the point where you would not be able to graduate on time and therefore were in danger of dropping out. Remember, this concept was created in 1906! Why do we wait until high school to identify at-risk students? Tradition? It cannot be because we are unable to identify these students earlier. Ask any teacher who has been in K–3 instruction with children for a few years and they will tell you without a doubt that they can identify potential dropouts long before middle school! Many teachers at the aforementioned at-risk education conferences wonder at the lack of elementary and middle school teacher attendees because they know that education has the ability to intervene much earlier than after children have literally sat through years of school being "behind"—some just waiting until they can drop out. Starting nearly a decade ago and utilizing input from literally hundreds of elementary and middle school teachers, NAREN has assembled and field-tested a simple instrument to make teachers both aware of the issues children are facing and provide leverage for taking action with an effective intervention program.

Selecting for Intervention at the Elementary School Level

Early Assessment of At-Risk Behaviors (EAARB) is a preliminary assessment for classroom teachers to determine if pre-school/primary children are probable for being at-risk of not succeeding (see Figure 17.1).

Figure 17.1. EAARB—Early Assessment of At-Risk Behaviors in Children.

E.A.A.R.B.
Early Assessment of At-Risk Behaviors in Children
Copyright 2010 © by Anthony Dallmann-Jones, PhD
Distributed by NAREN: www.NAREN.info

Date completed: _____ by _____

Check each one that applies for: _____/_____
                                         (Child's Name)   (Date of birth)

__ *Direct evidence of neglect
__ *Established evidence of abuse
__ *Sustained sadness and/or monitored for depression
__ *Known family history of abuse, neglect
__ *No one home when child arrives from school/left alone for long periods of time
__ *Poor school/academic performance
__ *Not reading by 3rd grade

PHYSICAL HEALTH:
__ Shots not complete, waived
__ Continual health problems
__ Comes to school hungry
__ Doesn't get good night's sleep/falls asleep in class
__ Low birth weight

HOME:
__ Lack of parental support
__ Hopeless, e.g., "My dad won't sign this."
__ Parent/family does not value education/schools
__ Pulled out for vacations or activities with no regard to time missed in school

---

(continued)

Figure 17.1 (continued). EAARB—Early Assessment of At-Risk
Behaviors in Children.

HOME (continued):
__ Missing 10 or more days in 1st semester
__ Two (or more) households, e.g., "Where do I go tonight?"
__ Little or no structure at home

PERSONAL:
__ Does not have many life experiences
__ Wants to be loved by anyone
__ Bargains for friendship
__ Gives up easily/needs teacher support
__ Emotionally immature for age in the classroom
__ Poor attitude toward school; doesn't care
__ Seeks teacher attention negatively
__ Disconcerted/flustered (almost lucky he/she got to school at all)
__ Angry
__ Lack of organizational skills
__ Lack of self-confidence

Scoring:

[Name of Child]_____

Circle appropriate category below.

Green—Warning:
Checking 1 *ed item
or
Checking 2 *or* 3 non-*ed symptoms

Orange—Danger:
Checking 2 *ed items
or
Checking 1 * item *and* 2 or more non-starred items

Red Zon—Critical:
Checking 3 or more *ed items
or
Checking 2* items *and* 3 or more non-* items

INTERPRETATION GUIDE

GREEN - WARNING—School personnel should be on alert and exhibit deliberate heightened awareness in watching for an increase in existing signs, or the addition of new ones. Weekly re-assessments with EAARB by a designated responsible professional are now warranted.

ORANGE - DANGER—School personnel should initiate a responsible and deliberate intervention to halt further damage to the child and to begin a specific recovery program.

RED ZONE - CRITICAL—School personnel should initiate a referral to the proper authority outside the school and begin an immediate collaborative effort with that/those agency(ies) in a strong intervention effort on behalf of the child.

Selecting for Intervention at the Middle School Level

Assessment of At-Risk Behaviors in Middle School (AARBMS) is a preliminary assessment to be used by teachers to determine if middle-level youth are probable for being at risk of not succeeding (see Figure 17.2).

Both the Early Assessment of At-Risk Behaviors in Children and the Assessment of At-Risk Behaviors in Middle School are available in licensed forms under "Books & Materials" on the NAREN website.

Figure 17.2. AARBMS—Assessment of At-Risk Behaviors in Middle School.

A.A.R.B.M.S.
Assessment of At-Risk Behaviors in Middle School
Copyright © 2010 by Anthony Dallmann-Jones, PhD
Distributed by NAREN: www.NAREN.info

Date completed: _____ by _____

Check each one that applies for: _____ / _____
       (Child's Name)   (Date of birth)

__ *Direct evidence of neglect
__ *Established evidence of abuse
__ *Sustained sadness and/or monitored for depression
__ *Known family history of abuse, neglect
__ *No one home when child arrives from school/left alone for long periods of time
__ *Poor school/academic performance
__ *Two years or more below grade level in reading
__ *Has been in possession of drugs, tobacco, weapons

PHYSICAL HEALTH:
__ Shots not complete, waived
__ Continual health problems
__ Doesn't get good night's sleep
__ Delayed physical development/growth (possibly from malnutrition)

HOME:
__ Lack of parental support
__ Hopeless
__ Parent/family does not value education/schools
__ Pulled out for vacations or activities with no regard to time missed in school
__ Missing 10 or more days in 1st semester
__ Unpredictable home base, e.g., "Where do I go tonight?"
__ Little or no structure at home (lack of positive consistent discipline)
__ Does no work outside of school (homework)

(continued)

Figure 17.2 (continued). AARBMS—Assessment of At-Risk Behaviors in
Middle School.

PERSONAL:
__ Does not have many life experiences
__ Wants to be loved by anyone
__ Bargains for friendship
__ Gives up easily/needs teacher support
__ Emotionally immature for age in the classroom
__ Poor attitude toward school; doesn't care
__ Seeks teacher attention negatively
__ Disconcerted/flustered (almost lucky he/she got to school at all)
__ Angry
__ Lack of organizational skills
__ Lack of self-confidence
__ Oversensitive to issues of fairness/injustice
__ Blames others habitually (external locus of control)
__ Cannot follow organizational system (lacks structure, realistic direction/focus)
__ Dirty/unkempt
__ Bullying behavior
__ Does not get along with others

Scoring:

[Name of Child]_____

Circle appropriate category below.

Green—Warning:
Checking 1 *ed item
or
Checking 2 *or* 3 non-*ed symptoms

Orange—Danger:
Checking 2 *ed items
or
Checking 1 * item *and* 2 or more non-starred items

Red Zon—Critical:
Checking 3 or more *ed items
or
Checking 2* items *and* 3 or more non-* items

INTERPRETATION GUIDE

GREEN - WARNING—School personnel should be on alert and exhibit deliberate heightened awareness in watching for an increase in existing signs, or the addition of new ones. Monthly re-assessments with AARBMS by a designated responsible professional are now warranted.

ORANGE - DANGER—School personnel should initiate a responsible and deliberate intervention to halt further damage to the child and to begin a specific recovery program.

RED ZONE - CRITICAL—School personnel should initiate a referral to the proper authority outside the school and begin an immediate collaborative effort with that/those agency(ies) in a strong intervention effort on behalf of the child.

Why Bother with Forms?

We need more paperwork—the right kind—on Shadow Children. We need utilitarian documentation because each year the child is with someone new; someone who does not know the child, but needs to! Referring back to the characteristics of excellent intervention programs, the first two characteristics are covered by the use of one of the following instruments: (1) clearly defined population, and (2) clearly defined precipitating behaviors. Note that we are not carrying forward a piece of "Hollenbacher material," that is, disparaging personal assaults on a child's character, but rather important clinical observations that acknowledge we have a child who may need intervention. There is way too much reinventing of the wheel in education, taking away from our valuable time with students. To find the succinct EAARB or AARBMS instrument in a student's jacket alerts the teacher to pay particular attention to symptomatic behaviors erupting, worsening, or dissipating.

Documentation provides leverage (proof) on behalf of the child. It clearly defines the problems that need to be addressed and allows the teachers and counselors to bring specific issues to the attention of the administration, for either continued surveillance or referral to agencies outside the school. Everyone is busy in the school environment, so how does one decide on priorities?

Children's needs come first. The reason for school is to address the needs of children. But which needs? Children are Pez dispensers of needs, so how does one select those to address? After all, there are only so many minutes in a day and so many dollars in the limited budget, and we need something we can honestly say helps to prioritize those needs. Documentation that says, "This child has a serious issue that needs to be addressed *now!*" shines a light on one of the finest moments in our profession—being a champion for a child.

CHAPTER 18

Preparing Teachers for Excellence in Educating the At-Risk Student

Is There a Need for a Concentrated Field of Study Called At-Risk Education?

NATIONAL awareness of the dropout issue is apparent to the U.S. Department of Education, which estimates that over 30 percent of today's youth are at risk of dropping out, and President Obama, who has announced that we have a "dropout crisis." Nine colleges and universities have also recognized the role that teacher-preparation institutions can play. Slowly but surely it has become apparent that effective school-staff training aimed at both at-risk prevention and intervention programming is a critical piece of the solution. Listed below are some of the programs and their approaches to at-risk education. These programs are currently active in educating teachers to prepare at-risk kids for life, including Marian University which is located in, of all places, Fond du Lac, Wisconsin. Marian University is the first university in the United States to offer an *accredited* Master's degree program in at-risk education.

Higher Education Institutions with Advanced Degree Programs in Alternative Education and/or At-Risk Education

The following program descriptions have been provided by a survey of higher education institutions that offer advanced degrees related to alternative education programming.

Marian University, Fond du Lac, WI
DIAL Program—Differentiated Instruction for Alternative Learners

The DIAL Program is an accredited, online Masters program. It began as a face-to-face program but the University quickly saw a national need for the program and broadened its scope. The DIAL Program prepares educators to more effectively meet the needs of at-risk/alternative students in the classroom. As part of its 30-credit program, graduate students design and conduct an action research project that prepares them to reach all students more effectively. DIAL graduate students are encouraged to become at-risk coordinators in their districts, teachers in their schools, and continue their effort to meet the needs of at-risk students. Upon completion of the DIAL Program graduates have the proper courses and hours to also earn Wisconsin's 952 Alternative Education Teacher license, qualifying them to teach across the curriculum.

Contact information:
Bob Bohnsack
Marian University
45 S. National Avenue
Fond du Lac, WI 54935
Tel: 1-800-2-Marian ext 8118
E-mail: bbohnsack@marianuniversity.edu
Web: http://soe.marianuniversity.edu

Gonzaga University—Spokane, WA
At-Risk Concentration Description

The Master of Arts in Teaching with concentration in Teaching At-Risk Students meets the needs of today's teachers who face multi-problematic issues in the classroom. The dynamics in the modern classroom are intensified by individual issues of each child. Family violence and child abuse, attention difficulties, emotional problems, and learning disabilities can greatly interfere with the student's academic and interpersonal performance. Teachers struggle with significant challenges for which they often have limited training and few resources. The Master of Arts in Teaching with concentration in Teaching At-Risk Students provides tools teachers need to reach their students. The courses in the concentration are based on research in the field of resiliency and asset development, offering a strength-based approach to student intervention.

Contact information:
Graduate Admissions Office
502 E Boone Ave, AD Box 25
Spokane, WA 99258-0025
Tel: 509.313.3481 or 509.313.3481
Toll free: 800.533.2554 or 800.533.2554 ext 6
Fax: 509.313.3491
E-mail: soegrad@gonzaga.edu

Harvard University—Cambridge, MA
Prevention Science and Practice

Prevention Science and Practice is dedicated to the practical application of contemporary research on risk, resilience, and prevention programming for children and adolescents in both school and out-of-school settings. The program focuses on how intervention and prevention practice, counseling, program development, consultation, leadership and research reduce the impact of risk faced by children and youth. The PSP master's degree is a self-contained program that trains prevention specialists in effective interventions to reduce risk and increase resiliency among children and youth. The EdM program can also serve as a foundation year for those who wish to pursue school social work/school adjustment or school counseling licensure through the Certificate of Advanced Study (CAS) in Counseling program.

Contact information:
Karen Bottari, Program Coordinator
Prevention Science and Practice Program
Harvard Graduate School of Education
607 Larsen Hall, 14 Appian Way
Cambridge, MA 02138
Tel: 617.495.4954
E-mail: bottarka@gse.harvard.edu
Web: http://www.gse.harvard.edu/academic/masters/psp/index.html

University of Pennsylvania—Lock Haven, PA
Alternative Education Studies Program

The Alternative Education Studies program makes it possible for education professionals to engage in reflective practice while improving teaching and program development skills. The program encourages exploration of methods, research, and epistemologies that focus on both the learner and systemic changes that will benefit all students. The Master of Education in Alternative Education is designed to support professionals in education and related fields. Students will develop skills, knowledge and competencies that will benefit them in their work in alternative and/or regular education settings.

The nation's first online program in alternative education offers innovative curriculum including a series of required and elective courses.

Contact information:
Nathaniel S. Hosley, Alternative Education Coordinator
Alternative Education Studies
Lock Haven University of Pennsylvania
Annex Building Lock Haven PA, 17745
Tel: 570.893.6247
Fax: 570.893.6248
Web: http://www.alted.lhup.edu

George Mason University—Fairfax, VA
Advanced Studies in Teaching and Learning (ASTL)

The 12-credit Education Core component of the Master's degree provides students with learning experiences and activities that simulate requirements for certification by the National Board for Professional Teaching Standards (NBPTS).

The Alternative Education Emphasis is an 18-credit component of the Master's degree, allowing students to specialize in Alternative Education.

Contact information:
Advanced Studies in Teaching and Learning
Graduate School of Education
George Mason University
4400 University Drive, 4B3

Robinson Hall A, 451
Fairfax, VA 22030-4444
Tel: 703.993.3640 or 703.993.2650
Fax: 703.993.9380
Web: http://gse.gmu.edu/programs/astl/

University of Wisconsin—Whitewater, WI
University of Wisconsin—Milwaukee, WI
Certificate in Teaching in Alternative Education Settings (TAES)

The TAES Program will assist licensed teachers and other professionals working with youth in recognizing and developing the knowledge, skills, and dispositions necessary to work in alternative educational settings. This online program consists of a sequence of four, two-credit courses and a one-credit, field-based experience. The program is designed so that participants can complete their program over one academic year or during the 12-week summer session.

Applicants for admission to this emphasis area must hold or be eligible for a regular teaching license in the State of Wisconsin for teaching in a public school. Exceptions to this policy may be made by the program coordinator on a case-by-case basis.

Contact information (Whitewater, WI):
University of Wisconsin—Whitewater
800 West Main St.
Whitewater, WI 53190
Web: http://www.uww.edu/gradstudies/postbachtaes.php

Dr. Anne Stinson, Program Coordinator
Tel: 262.472.1122
E-mail: stinsona@uww.edu

Dr. William Chandler, Program Coordinator
Tel: 262.472.5438
E-mail: chandelb@uww.edu

Contact information (Milwaukee, WI):
University of Wisconsin—Milwaukee
School of Education
Enderis Hall

2400 E. Hartford Ave.
Milwaukee, WI 53201
Tel: 414.229.4721
Web: http://www4.uwm.edu/soe/

Dr. Raquel Farmer-Hinton
Tel: 414.229.3320
E-mail: rfarhin@uwm.edu

Nicole Weber
Tel: 414.229.2326
E-mail: nicolea5@uwm.edu

Conclusion

What should be included in a program that prepares teachers to more effectively deal with at-risk students? The NAREN Nine Facets of Quality At-Risk Education listed in Chapter 16 suggests a solid framework for readers to, at the very least, launch a discussion. The NAREN Nine are based on the best research available on how to effectively reach and teach at-risk youth. It would behoove teacher training institutions and staff development programs to utilize the NAREN Nine as curricular scaffolding to reach and teach *all* students. The NAREN Nine are designed to be easy to employ and accommodating to the diversity naturally found in our population, the differences that make each child so irreplaceably unique and precious and the variances found in the resources of our communities and schools.

We toss around the word "standards" like a Frisbee. The NAREN Nine have likewise been called "standards," but they are a set of facets or aspects that make for a balanced and effective program-design tool. How many times have we seen yet another committee of educators going into session to design a program for "those kids" that is, unlike the Naren Nine, neither research-based nor based on effective practices? The question that begins with "*What* are we going to do . . ." can confidently be changed to "*How* are we going to do . . ." because the NAREN Nine successfully answers the *What* question. It is up to each school to decide *How* based on the needs of their particular population and the resources they have (or must gather) to implement their particular alternative program(s).

CHAPTER 19

Conclusion

A Concluding Statement for an Ongoing Problem

SUMMARIZING the complex issue of the Shadow Child Syndrome may cause this major problem to appear less significant than it really is. It is a problem with political as well as economic considerations and repercussions. It is a problem that demands a faster response in reacting to social considerations from the educational system—a system that responds sometimes much like the Titanic would if you had tried to change its course by pelting it with snowballs.

No matter what considerations are raised, it will always come down to, "What next?"

- "What next" is the educational system going to do in order to further join the fight and turn human suffering into human success?
- "What next" systemic changes should we make to improve our offerings to Shadow Children?
- "What next" effective programs and practices are we going to implement to compensate for those children coming to school with "shallow tool-and-skill boxes?"
- "What next" can we do to overcome the prejudice towards Shadow Children so that we remove the subconscious as well as deliberate blockages that sometimes prevent us from making the adjustments necessary to match systemic offerings to student needs?

We don't have all the answers. But we do have a lot of the answers. An important question is this: If we have so many answers, why aren't schools changing their practices? This is not just an interesting and necessary question to answer; it is a very straightforward attempt to solve the "curriculum-lock" problem. Here are some possible answers to this question.

1. *Perhaps we didn't know it was that big of a problem.* A former elementary and middle school teacher, who for over a decade has been the education correspondent for a major national media presence, was alarmed when he was apprised of the at-risk statistics in this book. "I had no idea this problem was so extensive!" He is a person in the know, a concerned, well-educated man who tries to keep up with all that is going on in education in the United States. He did not know.

This is one reason this book calls at-risk youth Shadow Children. It is much like how the shadow economy of the United States (taxes evaded, production and trade of illicit drugs, bartered goods, household production, and unregulated micro-enterprise) has huge implications for the nation's Gross National Product—but who knows how extensive and how much the impact is? Therefore, how many people talk about this issue or desire to do anything about it?

We are all ignorant about the full impact of a Shadow Children population until we become informed. This book is aimed straight at removing ignorance as a reason for not being concerned.

2. *Perhaps we just don't know what to do even if we realize the scope of the problem.* While visiting a lot of schools and teaching a lot of teachers of at-risk students I learn a lot about the inside reasons why we can't implement necessary changes: money shortages, staff indifference, school board members more concerned with getting revenge than making a positive difference for kids, administrative politics, and more. But I run into just a few teachers and administrators who state that they not only see avenues of implementation but they are also doing something to make that difference. As long as there are some, there is good reason to hope. These few are our role models, our mentors, and our guiding light.

As an example, on the NAREN website (in the members-only Program Profiles database) there are dozens of programs and classroom practices listed and described that work well with at-risk youth. These are tried and true programs and practices, not whimsical or hopeful ideas. These are field-tested and battle-ready programs and practices. So it will not be for lack of knowledge of effective programs and practices that we forestall action.

3. *Perhaps we do not know how to design or structure prevention and intervention efforts to stem this tide of failure and suffering in our young people.* Mentioned in this book are three scaffoldings including the NAREN Self-Study Kit, Positive Youth Development guidelines, and Lynn Stoddard's Educating for Human Greatness that basically tell us what to do in order to establish a meaningful and effective program for Shadow Children. Yes, it takes systemic and sustained planning and effort to make a dent, but the architectural plans are in existence to guide the direction of that effort, meanwhile eliminating a lot of wasted resources and frustration.

4. *Perhaps we don't care (feel) enough to know enough.* As a former psychotherapist and owner of a counseling office, we dealt with some tough cases of people repeating behaviors despite their destructive and apparent consequences. Some of these people were sent to us by a judge who had told them: "Therapy or jail, take your pick!" Some came because a relative told them they either had to get help or the relationship was over: "I see you drunk one more time and the kids and I are gone!" Some came because their boss made them: "Get help or get another job!" Rarely in our office did we see anyone overcome their habits because of warnings or threats. Occasionally, I would get quite blunt with people who expressed varied excuses for why they either had no problem, had no good reason to quit, or relapsed more often than not. I would simply say, "You are not hurting enough yet. The pity is that not only might you take yourself down permanently while bottoming out, but you will more than likely take your associates and loved ones with you. For your and their sakes, I hope you find your least endurable pain soon. Come back when you do."

This *threshold factor* is indeed a mystery. There was a railroad crossing near my childhood home in Ohio back in the 1960s that just had the old wooden black and white X sign as a warning: East Town Road. Seven people, one by one, were eventually killed there by trains. After the seventh death they finally put up red flashing warning lights at that crossing. I ask myself even today: Why seven? I mean, why after the second death didn't someone say, "Hey, human life is precious. If it had been my wife or child or husband or parent dying on that crossing, in retrospect, I certainly would have found it worthwhile to spend the county tax dollars on a warning light prior to that night!" Why not after three? Why not after four, five, six? No, it looks like *in that* case it took seven deaths. Seven people needlessly wiped out, and seven sets of families and friends suffering seemed to be enough to tip the county cash drawer into proactivity about that crossing light.

Yet, in the same state, one guy died of an overdose of drinking Everclear (a 190-proof alcohol beverage) and the state outlawed it almost instantly. I guess the magic number of Everclear deaths is one. In the Chicago-area Tylenol scare of 1982, seven people mysteriously and randomly died within a few days of one another from cyanide-laced pills placed in retail containers by a murderous individual(s). Now *everything* we buy is tamper-proof. One incident again creates massive change. Yet we have people dying right and left from lung cancer and still allow cigarettes to be sold. People dying in drunken-related highway slaughter (over 42,000 a year in the United States and increasing yearly) is not enough to deter the 120,000,000 drivers who annually self-report driving under the influence of alcohol, nor has it created the legislation necessary to *stop* alcohol-related deaths. (If only the number seven would work in the DWI category!)

5. *Maybe we didn't know just how expensive it was to NOT do anything.* One purpose of this book was to assist in bringing the "expense account of denial" into focus, as shown in Chapter 2. It costs almost as much to not address the Shadow Child problem as it would to *annually* rebuild and secure five Afghanistans and five Iraqs, according to The Every Child Matters Educational Fund (2003). They also point out in their findings:

  • For every $1 invested in after-school programs, $3 come back through reduced juvenile crime and improved school performance.
  • For every $1 invested in quality pre-kindergarten programs that improve school readiness, society gets $7 in benefits.

These statistics drive home the "pay me now, or pay me a *whole lot more* later" concept fairly well. What is left? Could there possibly be some other solid reason why we do not launch effective efforts we need to reduce our Shadow Child population?

6. *Perhaps we are prejudiced against Shadow Children!* Once we have

removed all the overt reasons for not being more systematically and financially dedicated to supporting our Shadow Children, what is left except this uncomfortable psychological conclusion? We love to exhibit our forefinger and thumb at right angles to each other on our forehead and exclaim, "Loser!" We only want to see winners. No one remembers who finished second last year in the Boston Marathon, or who was the runner up in NBA standings in 2005, or who lost the Stanley Cup two years ago (unless it was your team).

If the former President thinks at-risk kids cannot learn, if the general populace thinks of Shadow Children as a pain in their side, if we can only lament on how much money it costs us for the special programs and teachers to remediate, if we look down our noses at the less fortunate, if we blame these children for the circumstances they did not create, if we wish they would all just go away, we need to do two things:

1. We need to wake up our intellect and learn enough to care enough. To that end, the Bibliography provides a great deal of helpful information.
2. We need to wake up our empathic feelings and experience about what it must feel like to already have two strikes against you, and then to go into a school that sighs and/or sneers at you as if you were a lower-caste member. These children need reassurance, hope, and enlightened programs and personnel from the profession. They need the proof of action that they matter, and that they are worthy of rescuing.

Many inaccurately think that prejudice is based on not knowing enough about your object of prejudice. In actuality, *prejudice is thinking you know enough when you don't.* You overcome prejudice by getting close to and familiar with your object of prejudice, rather than distancing yourself. I ask my graduate students (who are also teachers) the following question: "How do you learn to like the most dislikable of your students?"

Then I pose an answer to them:

Look into their eyes, see the real child, invite them to come out,
Look past symptoms, speak to the causes, hurts, fears, and self-doubt,
Withhold your judgments of the obvious exterior view,
For underneath that child's surface is someone ... just ... like ... you.

It is my hope, and the goals of the National At-Risk Education Network, to awaken us to an understanding of this nation's number one domestic issue *and* to point out productive avenues of intervention and prevention, *and* to care enough to take action so that all children can succeed in school and at life. We need hope, good information, collaboration, and unified, persistent effort to solve this problem in order to help those who are often confused, misdirected, and/or lost. This book was written with that in mind as a contributing part of the beacon to point the way.

The Secret Angel Club

A dear friend of mine, Steve Hartley, tells of the results of a study he did in 2002 with Shadow Children who dropped out in Madison, Wisconsin. Almost every single dropout that was interviewed felt that no one in authority ever noticed them; they never felt connected to the school, and this was one of their major reasons for leaving school.

This is preventable. Some things may not be. Some things may be difficult to overcome. But that Shadow Children are not noticed? This is a black eye made blacker by the fact that it is preventable. We can do something about this, and by next week! It is called The Secret Angel Club, and here is how it is set up.

- Elect a Secret Angel Club coordinator.
- Secretly identify Shadow Children in the school.
- Recruit Secret Angel Club members—any adult in the school can be one if they are willing to commit 10 minutes a month to change a child's life. Sometimes custodial people make the best Secret Angels!
- Pair a Secret Angel with at least one child. Don't overload your Secret Angel. Note: A designated child must not be enrolled in the classroom of a Secret Angel teacher.
- At one point, during every week or two, the Secret Angel should make eye contact with the child and say something positive and/or smile. Suggestions are:

"Well, hi there, Susie!" (With a look of pleasant discovery)
"Oh, Bob, you look super today!"
"Hey, Linda, how's it going?"
"Well, doesn't Chantall look terrific today!"
"There you are, Harold! I was wondering if I would see you today!"

- It's the direct eye contact and welcoming body language that makes the difference. Sometimes a big smile and a hand wave will do, particularly if it is awkward to use words in certain surroundings.
- Make a point of "finding" the child in different places of the school.
- Spice it up and think of ways you can make the child's day special in subtle ways.
- Avoid giving gifts of any kind. Your caring attitude is enough.
- Do not share with anyone else (besides other Secret Angels) who your child is by name.

Classifying Abuse and Neglect

Why *Is* Abuse Harmful?

THIS question may appear silly to ask, but not when you consider how prevalent abuse is, and has been, down through time. Millions have justified abuse, often righteously. Just think of the many clichs: "The best defense is a good offense" (and, of course, I have the right to defend myself!); "Spare the rod and spoil the child" (and nobody will like the child if it's spoiled so I'm doing it a favor!); "This hurts me worse than it does you" (it's your good fortune that you have someone willing to suffer in order to teach you such a valuable lesson!); "We must have order" (and there just is no better way to achieve this order than to punish you!).

When you read the CSCAN list in this Appendix it becomes apparent that there is practically no end to abuse. We are, like the fish, immersed in it to such a degree that we no longer notice it. Despite all the laws, commandments, morals, ethics, and poetry pleadings down through the years, we still have a plethora of abuse occurring on a nearly constant basis. It seems almost legitimate to say, "Come on, let's be honest. Abuse is a way of life, we just have all these little 'rules' to keep it under control. Just don't get caught and it's no big deal. Don't be so naive."

Indeed, just what is so bad about abuse? Answer: It goes against the *Plan*—the plan of actualizing our human destiny, of achieving a natural state of lightness, sensitivity, beauty, health, and intelligent concern for self and others. In other words, it suppresses and limits human potential. If there was such a thing as a psychological sin, then smothering a human being's potential would be it.

It is proposed by some that the ultimate human-body purpose is to reach a state of consistent spirituality. If that is true, or is at least supposed to be true, it is very difficult to acquire this blissful harmonious state and participate in abusive behaviors at the same time. It is simply a law of physics that two things cannot occupy the same space at the same time. Abuse and spirituality cannot occupy the same human at the same time or, better stated, one cannot express one's positive spiritual nature while being abusive. It is also very difficult to express one's spirituality while allowing oneself to be abused.

Abuse is incongruent with human destiny. That is the major reason (among many) that abuse is painful.

> Don't ever forget, Miss Radha: "To the senseless, nothing is more maddening than sense. Pala is a small island completely surrounded by twenty-nine hundred million mental cases. In the country of the insane the integrated man doesn't become King." Mr. Bahu's face was positively twinkling with Voltairean glee. "He gets lynched!" (Aldous Huxley, *Island*, p.78)

Because history seems to verify that abuse is habitual doesn't make it sane or humane. Abuse is destructive because one can never be deeply, satisfyingly, healthfully, harmoniously, and genuinely human in the midst of abuse. Most people, it seems, want a wholesome, peaceful lifestyle more than anything. They started out as innocent, genuine, loving, spontaneous humans as babies—then lost these positive characteristics due to abuse. They can get them back by saying "No" to abuse in any form, by recovering from abusive patterns that have been internalized as coping mechanisms, and by learning all they can about this accepted destructive philosophy of nihilism.

Relationships of Abuse Forms

The potential negative consequence of all abuse/neglect is a rupture in the victim's relationship with his or her pristine self. This creates a dynamic in which all forms of abuse/neglect can ultimately result in spiritual abuse—damaging the primary and foundational relationship with Self. This explains why sexual abuse often creates the deepest damage in the individual.

Sexual abuse interferes directly with our identity, because primarily we identify ourselves by our gender. The first thing everyone wants to know when a newborn arrives is its gender. This is so that "it" can be related to as an individual identity. The very foundation of personality formation rests upon gender in our society. Sexual abuse casts shame and doubt upon the manner by which the victim relates with his/her own core personality orientation. This can have pervasive and long-term damaging consequences for the victim in all his/her future relationships.

Likewise, emotional abuse is very powerful because emotions are both physical and mental and provide the psychosomatic link between mind and body. Thus, emotional abuse is two-pronged and affects all parts of the victim's world. Note: A special case of social abuse, triangulation, is included in Appendix II because of its prevalence as a vehicle for a variety of abuse patterns (and because it seems to be rampant in faculty lounges).

Classification System of Child Abuse and Neglect

The Value of a Nomenclature

The overall benefit of a nomenclature, such as the Classification System of Child Abuse and Neglect (CSCAN), is that it provides information regarding the potential impact of specific child-raising behaviors. It partially answers the question, "How are Shadow Children created? CSCAN also provides a clear and organized means for communication about, as well as substantiation and documentation of, abuse and neglect.

A very worthwhile expenditure of America's tax dollars has gone into publishing a directory of not only federal (general) definitions, but of each state's definitions. All are listed in a free, 93 page booklet, *Definitions of Child Abuse and Neglect: Summary of State Laws,* which can be found online at the Child Welfare Information Gateway (www. childwelfare.gov/systemwide/laws_policies/statutes/defineall.pdf). The Child Welfare Information Gateway is a wonderful service provided by the Children's Bureau, which is part of the Administration for Children and Families at the U.S. Department of Health and Human Services.

Note: It is important to remember that, psychologically speaking, abuse and neglect are *subjectively validated* experiences. Any legal proceedings for affixing culpability are utilized only to objectify what the victim has known since the moment of violation. In other words, you do not have to "provide proof" to the victim. They were there.

The compilation that makes up CSCAN was originally proposed in my book, *Resolving Unfinished Business: Assessing the Effects of Being Raised in a Dysfunctional Environment* (1996), and has since been validated and modified through utilization by numerous school systems, clinics, counselors, and treatment centers.

So-called verbal abuse is not included as a separate category in CSCAN because, technically, words are tools or methods of conveyance of other forms of abuse. Words are often used to create mental and emotional abuse. Yelling "Fire!" in a crowded restaurant would be a verbal vehicle for physical abuse. Sexual abuse can also be verbally transmitted; for instance, one can denigrate a person sexually by ridiculing his or her genitalia or gender.

Classification System of Child Abuse and Neglect (CSCAN)

Physical Abuse (PA)
PA.___

01. Deliberate attempted murder
02. Slapping with the hand (not spanking)
03. Shaking with rapid movement
04. Scratching with the fingers
05. Pinching with the fingers
06. Squeezing painfully
07. Hitting with the fist
08. Spanking
09. Pulling hair
10. Beating with objects, (boards, sticks, belts, kitchen utensils, yardsticks, electric cords, shovels, fan belts, hoses, etc.)
11. Throwing
12. Shoving
13. Slamming against walls or objects
14. Utilizing temperature extremes:
    a. burning
    b. scalding
    c. freezing
15. Forcing of food
16. Forcing of water
17. Forcing of objects into orifices (does not include sexual abuse)
18. Utilizing objects to pinch, poke or scratch

19. Painful tickling
20. Overworking

Physical Neglect (PN)
PN.___

01. Attempted murder via willful preoccupation (allowing a person to enter a life-threatening situation with the intent he/she will be fatally injured)
02. Lack of essentials:
    a. food
    b. water
    c. clothing
    d. shelter
03. Leaving the child alone in age-inappropriate ways
04. Leaving a child who is too young in charge of others
05. Failure to provide medical care
06. Allowing or encouraging the use of alcohol and/or other drugs
07. Failure to protect the child from the abuse of others
08. Failure to protect the child from the abuse of the spouse

Emotional Abuse (EA)
EA.___

01. Double binds (a deliberately perpetrated predicament where all choices given the child are negative ones)
02. Projection and transfer of adult problems onto the child (scapegoating)
03. Alterations of child's reality (lying) (e.g., "Dad's not drunk, he's just tired.")
04. Overprotecting (does not healthfully allow child to experience consequences of its own actions)
05. Enmeshment, or smothering with apparent affection but in actuality, living through the child.
06. Preventing the child from learning appropriate developmental tasks (trust, autonomy, initiative, industry, etc.)
07. Double messages [e.g., "Of course, I love you, dear." (said as Mom tenses up and grimaces); "I love you just as you are, you just need to

change a couple of traits."; "I love spending time with you, I just have to run right now."; and so on.]

08. Not acknowledging that abuse or neglect has taken place

09. Using child for personal gain (e.g., financial profit, holding on to a spouse, providing a sense of meaning for the parent, etc.)

Emotional Neglect (EN)
EN.___

01. Desertion or abandonment
02. Failure to nurture, care for, or love the child
03. Failure to provide structure or set limits
04. Not listening to, hearing, or believing the child
05. Expecting the child to provide unreasonable emotional nurturing to adults instead of receiving it
06. Deliberately withdrawing or withholding love
07. Caregivers not being emotionally present due to:
    a. mental illness
    b. chemical dependency
    c. depression
    d. compulsivity in themselves
    e. compulsivity in the family environment
    f. extended physical illness
08. Excessive guilting (dwelling on mistakes)
09. Excessive shaming (characterizing the child as flawed, defective, a "mistake," or at fault for existing)
10. Sarcasm (sideways anger)
11. Inflicting unreasonable fear
12. Minimizing the child's emotions ("You shouldn't feel sad, angry, afraid, happy, etc.")

Mental Abuse (MA)
MA.___

01. Excessive blaming (overloaded with criticism)
02. Degrading
03. Name calling

04. Put-downs by comparisons
05. Excessive teasing
06. Making fun of, laughing at, belittling
07. Nagging or haranguing
08. Screaming
09. Verbal assault (frequent "jackhammer" barrages of words)
10. Manipulating, deceiving, tricking (deliberate misleading)
11. Betraying
12. Cruelty
13. Intimidating, threatening, bullying
14. Controlling or overpowering
15. Not taking child's thoughts seriously
16. Put-downs via patronizing
17. Discrediting (not giving credit where it is due)
18. Disapproving of child's individuality
19. Making light of or minimizing wants, needs
20. Raising hopes falsely, breaking promises
21. Responding inconsistently or arbitrarily
22. Making vague demands
23. Saying "If only you were [better or different]."
24. Denigrated because of gender, ethnic, religious, or racial differences

Mental Neglect (MN)
MN.___

01. Lack of communication skills development
02. Lack of praise or encouragement to develop intellectually
03. Undereducation
04. Lack of affirmation regarding uniqueness

Sexual Abuse (SA)
SA.___

01. Forced rape
02. Fondling, inappropriate touching
03. Sexual harassment, innuendoes, jokes, comments

04. Leering
05. Exposing self to
06. Masturbating in front of
07. Mutual masturbation
08. Oral sex
09. Anal sex
10. Intercourse
11. Penetration with fingers
12. Penetration with objects
13. Stripping/exposing
14. Sexual punishments
15. Inappropriate or excessive enemas
16. Pornography: taking inappropriate pictures and/or forcing the child to watch
17. Coercing children to have sex with each other
18. Forced sexual activity with animals
19. Inappropriate invasion of bathroom/bedroom privacy

Sexual Neglect (SN)
SN.___

01. Failure to educate children concerning healthy sexual limits and boundaries
02. Failure to educate children concerning menstruation, conception, pregnancy, birth control, sexually transmitted diseases, and so on.
03. Failure to help children differentiate intimacy issues from sexual issues
04. Failure to help children develop positive self-esteem regarding their sexual selves

Vicarious Abuse (VA)
VA.___

Vicarious abuse is a special case of abuse in which the victim is part of a family or other system where someone else is abused in some way. The witnessing of abuse (PA, EA, MA, SA) can be just as damaging as being the actual recipient of the abuse.

You may acquire from NAREN the latest version of the CSCAN assessment form as a reproducible master copy for your school's assessment needs, along with a written statement of a release to use it. It can be ordered online at the NAREN website (go to www.AtRiskEducation.net and look under under "Books & Materials") for the cost of the envelope and postage. It's free, in other words.

When ordering, please include the name(s) and address(es) of the school(s) where the form will be utilized. This is for our records, so that we can imprint the specific school name and address on each master copy. Purchase orders are welcome.

A Case Study in Commonality

Triangulation

THIS section clearly defines a frequently socialized pattern of abuse in homes, schools, and businesses. Triangulation serves as an example of just how ordinary and socially acceptable certain forms of abuse and neglect have become. It is also poignant to note that aspects of the Shadow Child Syndrome may be active in the personalities of teachers as well as in students. The height of professionalism includes confronting the self first.

I extend a warm thanks to Marsha Utain and Barb Oliver for the clarity they bring to this common pattern of toxic human interaction.

A Common and Complex Form of Social Abuse

The Drama Triangle is the representation of a complex interactional process involving the three participating roles of Victim, Persecutor, and Rescuer. The Triangle is based on blame and guilt and is put into operation whenever any type of lie or denial occurs. Without blame, guilt, or lies there can be no Drama Triangle and no chaos. Instead, there would be healthy, responsible relationships based on honest and clear communications. If a family, faculty, organization, or office wishes to function in a healthy manner, offering support and development to its members, triangulation must be eliminated. It will take awareness and persistent determination.

Victim

The Victim position is the key role in the Triangle because it is the position around which the others revolve. People operating in the

Victim position take no responsibility for their actions or feelings. They truly believe that they are life's "fall guys," and that everyone in the world is "doing it to them." They continually look for someone or something else to blame for things not working in their lives. Victims can frequently be identified by their use of such language as "Everyone/anyone does it to me," "You/they (the government, mother, father, boss, spouse, children, and so on) do it to me," and "Poor me."

There are two basic types of Victims: the Pathetic Victim, and the Angry Victim. The Pathetic Victim plays the pity ploy, using woeful, poor-me looks and the desolate language of self pity, while the Angry Victim pretends to be powerful, using angry statements such as "I won't let you do it to me," "Look what you did to me," or "You're bad."

Both types of Victim are looking for someone to blame for the emotions they are having and for their lives not working. In addition, they are looking for a Rescuer, someone they can hook into taking care of them and their responsibilities.

Rescuer

As any recovering co-alcoholic knows, the role of the Rescuer is a highly addictive role because it is the position of the Good Guy. Because of the way most people are raised, whenever they feel guilty they have learned to get out of the guilt by moving into the Rescuer/Good Guy position. People do not like to be labeled the Bad Guy so they actively seek the position of Rescuer and, because it affords them some relief from pain, they become addicted to it.

We are raised from birth to believe that we must be good. We are trained by the standards of our parents, churches, and society that in order to be good we must take care of other people physically, emotionally, or spiritually, even at the cost of our own being. Drilled into many of us is the idea that to take care of oneself is to be selfish which, of course, is seen as bad. Therefore, when the Victim approaches us with blame or tales of woe, we are already prime targets for the manipulative hook of guilt. We already believe that we should take care of other people's problems and that if we do not we are bad. By refusing to help we fear that we will be seen as abandoning someone in distress. Because we do not wish to be cast in the Bad Guy/Persecutor role we jump in to rescue the Victim, even when it is not in our best interests.

If a child did not do what the parent wanted, then the child was labeled bad and cast in the role of the Persecutor. Taking the position of Rescuer, therefore, affords a person some relief from guilt and gives the person the opportunity to pretend they are acting unselfishly and for someone else's good. This creates the momentary high that makes the Rescuer position addictive. The Rescuer does not realize that, perhaps subconsciously, they are being motivated by selfish reasons. They just do not want to feel like or appear to be a bad person.

There is another important point to understand about Rescuers in the Drama Triangle. Because of the very nature of the Triangle, Rescuers must have a Victim; someone to take care of, someone to control, someone who, by their very need, makes the Rescuer feel good. When people are codependent and therefore addicted to the Rescuer role, they will find that they have a need to rescue. In order to fill that need, they need a Victim they can help. If there isn't one available the Rescuer may attempt to create one.

Example: You leave the store and while walking to the car notice that you were shortchanged 10¢ by the checkout lady. You remark about this to a friend and laugh about it.

Your friend says, "You shouldn't put up with that. I would raise hell!"

You respond, "Ah, it's only a dime and I am sure it was an innocent oversight."

Your friend continues. "Well, I hear they are always shortchanging people at this store. I think you should confront them!"

You stop walking, thinking, "Yeah, she's right. I don't want to appear to be a victim."

Your friend insists. "Aren't you going to do something? A dime here and a dime there, if they do that to every other shopper you know how much they are putting in their pockets at the end of the day?"

You are still on the fence.

Your friend, pulling the trigger, says, "If you want to be a victim or are too yellow, I will do it for you. Give me the receipt. It is time someone set them straight. It is always us 'little people' who pay for crime!"

This friend is trying hard to create a Victim, and has invented the righteous Rescuer role for herself, completely out of thin air. See how simple it is? And it creates a story that she can tell over and over to people every time someone mentions that store's name or is shortchanged, or when she needs to verify to others what a noble person she is. And your name will be part of that story. Forever.

In general, Rescuers need to be needed, and they need to be in control and be *right* no matter what the cost. Being in control and being right allows the Rescuer to avoid dealing with his or her own unresolved emotions or problems. In all addictions the substance or behavior (in this case, rescuing) is used by the addict to avoid feelings.

Persecutor

The role of the Persecutor is the role of the Bad Guy, the Villain. It is the one role that few people consciously choose as their starting place in the Triangle. In fact, it is the role that keeps the Triangle going because people in the Triangle are attempting to avoid this position by moving into the Rescuer role or by perceiving themselves as Victims. No one likes to see themselves as bad. Even convicted felons want to be seen as Victims of society, rather than society's Persecutors. The Persecutor role is the one that Victims use, along with blame, to maneuver others into rescuing them. What makes the Persecutor position very interesting is the fact that once you are in the Triangle and you decide to leave it, you must leave from this position. In other words, when you remove yourself from playing the game of triangulation, anyone still playing will usually perceive you as the Persecutor: "Here I am in need and you walk away! Thanks a *lot!*" "Just when she needed him most he left. What a #@&*. Men are all alike. They only care about themselves!"

Positioning, Maneuvering, and Rules in the Triangle

Key points worth remembering about the Triangle:

1. *The Triangle is based on lies.* Tell a lie to yourself or someone else, whether it is a lie about data or a lie about your emotions or your experience, and you move immediately into the Triangle and the addictive process.
2. *All shoulds are a lie.* Therefore, shoulds will throw you into the Triangle. (An important piece of the healing process is learning how to go about getting your needs and wants met after you learn to distinguish them from your shoulds, or the things that other people have told you are your needs.)
3. *All positions in the Triangle cause pain.* No matter what position you are in at any given moment in the Triangle, you will be in some form of discomfort or pain.

4. *There is no power in the Triangle.* When you are in the Triangle you are operating from powerlessness and irresponsibility, no matter what position you are playing.

5. *Everyone has a favorite starting position.* It is usually either the Rescuer or the Victim. Few people choose the Persecutor as a starting position.

6. *Once you are hooked into the Triangle, you will end up playing all the positions.* Because of the nature of the Triangle, this happens whether you like it or not. You may perceive yourself as a Rescuer who wound up as someone's Victim while at the same time that person perceives you as the Persecutor.

7. *Guilt is the experience that hooks you into the Triangle.* Some points on guilt:

   - Guilt is a signal that someone is pulling you into the Triangle.
   - In order to stay out of the Triangle you need to learn to give yourself permission to feel guilty without acting on that guilt. In other words, do not let guilt push you into the Rescuer position.
   - Learn to sit with the guilt and be uncomfortable. This particular type of guilt is not the same as that of being out of integrity as a result of having broken a rule, moral, or law.

8. *The escape hatch out of the Triangle is located at the Persecutor position.* Telling the truth and feeling your emotions opens the escape hatch leading out of the Triangle. In other words, in order to leave the Triangle or, for that matter, stay out of it you have to be willing for others (the Victims or the other Rescuers) to perceive you as the Bad Guy, then go through whatever emotions surface as a result of their perception. This does not mean that you are the Bad Guy, it just means that others choose to see you that way. If you are not willing to be seen as a Persecutor, you will get hooked into rescuing and keep yourself in the Triangle. Again, if you are already in the Triangle and wish to leave, you have to be willing for the others in the Triangle to see you as the Persecutor.

9. *You can play The Drama Triangle with yourself.* Once you have been raised in a dysfunctional family, you do not need anyone else to push you into the Triangle!

   - The way you play The Drama Triangle by yourself is by listening to the negative voices inside your head that beat you up, put you down and constantly "should" on you. Remember, shoulds are a lie. They have nothing to do with who you really are. They are someone else's interpretation of what to do and what is good.

- When you play The Drama Triangle with yourself, your "should-er" will persecute you so that you will feel like the Victim. At the same time you will be feeling guilty. This will trigger the belief that you are the Persecutor. The guilt will drive you to rescue someone (or some situation), even when no one except you is there attempting to manipulate you into the Rescuer position.

10. *When you actively participate in a relationship with someone who lives in the Triangle, you must be aware of the hooks.* It is difficult to be around people who constantly operate in the Triangle and not get hooked in yourself, especially if your personal boundaries are not clear and you have not learned to recognize the Triangle.

11. *Your internalized "should-er" is also the voice that pushes you into the Triangle when others around you are already in and attempting to hook you.* The "should-er" is the false self, the part that is actually someone else you believe to be you. It is controlling, negative, rigid, perfectionistic, and righteous. Without this part of you operating, you could not participate in the Triangle.

12. *Being in the Triangle is not being alive; it is a living death.* It is a life of pain, inauthenticity, and a lack of love and acceptance.

13. *Suicide is the ultimate Victim act, the ultimate act of self pity.* When the Victim perceives they cannot get anyone to come to the rescue anymore and they do not have the courage to seek new alternatives, they may turn to suicide.

14. *Telling the truth and experiencing your emotions is the only way out of the Triangle.* To do that you have to learn to know and define your boundaries, and take care of responsibility for recognizing, experiencing, expressing, and completing your emotions.

Avoiding the Triangle

To stay out of the Triangle, learn to tell the truth about what emotions you are feeling and take responsibility for them. Remember that no one else is responsible for your emotions. No one else can fix them for you or change them for you. People may support you in experiencing them, but ultimately no one but you can complete and release your emotions.

Frequently, dysfunctional families are so repressive that you cannot identify certain emotions or distinguish them from other types of experiences. When you (1) tell the truth about what you are feeling, (2) no longer take on the guilt that others try to place on you, and (3) are willing to feel the fear and sadness when accused of being the Persecutor by people who stay in the Triangle, you will step out of the chaos in your life. By being responsible and acknowledging and experiencing your emotions, you are also being responsible for any addiction you may have, and this is the first big step to recovery.

When you are further along in your healing process, you will be able to recognize your various emotions. Then you will begin to express them to others in order to get further in touch with these emotions, and not as an attempt to make someone else responsible for them. Remember: This is a process, and you may slide back and forth along the *denial/acceptance* continuum until you are truly and completely in touch with your emotions.

Prevention as Early Intervention

The 4R Elementary Curriculum

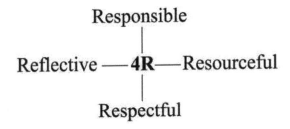

THE 4R Curriculum prepares youth to live well and succeed in the twenty-first century. It is progressive and individually tailored to students, thereby providing a ready model for inclusion, discouraged learners, and other individually needs-based curriculum efforts. It can overlay any content-oriented curriculum and magnifies its effectiveness by adding meaning and applauding individual perspectives as an integral part of the curriculum.

The 4R Curriculum induces willingness in students because of its unique and individualized nature. It can also be adapted to an online presence for homebound or isolated students. It was inevitable that such a model as the 4R Curriculum would be developed, as it is more in line with student needs and interests. As always, adequate field-testing is called for in order to fine tune the model for the full power of its programs to become actualized. Valid field-testing of the 4R Curriculum with willing students will establish this program similarly for the reluctant learner based on the strength of experience, confidence in the material, and best-suited practices.

The 4R Curriculum is a K–12 curriculum designed to promote healthy, vibrant, and productive students who will be empowered (have tools and skills) to promote enthusiastic lives for themselves, their families and society. Fundamental training in progressive thinking, physical conditioning, and technological, social and economic skills are the platform of the curriculum. The 4R Curriculum borrows liberally from new paradigmatic areas in education such as multiple intelligences and realities, emotional intelligence, and is infused with a major thrust in computer skills and global education via the Internet.

Students of the 4R Curriculum are prepared in four major character areas: Warrior, Friend, Citizen, and Philosopher. These four areas represent Resourcefulness, Respect, Responsibility, and Reflection. For younger children these areas are represented by the Tiger, Wolf, Porpoise, and Owl. Students are immersed in all four character areas throughout the 4R Curriculum, with flexibility for them to major in one or more in order to suit their needs, goals, and particular personalities. Other character areas can be negotiated.

RESOURCEFUL
stamina
content-area knowledge
computer skills
problem-solving skills
choice-making skills
conflict-resolution skills
money management
creativity—esthetics
strong identity → confidence → success cycle
resiliency

The Warrior

RESPONSIBLE
internal locus of control
healthfully interdependent
self-initiating
determination
collaborative skills
community service restitution

The Citizen

RESPECTFUL
non-abusive
compassionate
charitable
concerned
empathic
restorative justice

The Friend

REFLECTIVE
critical thinker
cognitively savvy
accepting of multiple viewpoints
insightful
meditational
global consciousness

The Philosopher

The 4R Elementary Classroom

The 4R Curriculum classroom is envisioned as a mentally, socially, emotionally, and physically active classroom. Constructivist and project-oriented modes are prevalent, with individual needs-based assessments being continually performed by the teacher. Student assessment is via electronic and tangible portfolios. Lectures by teachers are limited to 10 minutes, as most learning is socially or individually orientated. One suggestion is to (after explaining the 4R Curriculum to students) set up a point system whereby each student must have a certain number of points per week from each of the four categories. Particular numbers for each student are negotiated and contracted with the teacher on an individually prescribed basis.

Prevalent learning strategies in a 4R classroom might be:

- Community Service
- Computer-Assisted Instruction
- Contract Learning
- Cooperative Learning
- Discovery
- Discussion
- Field Trips

- Internet Education
- Learning Centers
- Learning Packets
- Peer Teaching
- Projects
- Resource People
- Simulation
- Student Research

Conclusion

The personalized curriculum, inherent flexibility of the program, and the project and constructivist orientation of the 4R Curriculum permits a matching of student interests, needs, and abilities with curricular content, thereby reducing boredom, disinterest, and discipline problems. More importantly, the opportunities for success—the reason a classroom exists in the first place—are greatly increased.

Bibliography and Readings

Administration for Children and Families, Office of Planning, Research and Evaluation, U.S. Department of Health and Human Services. (2004). *National Survey of Child and Adolescent Well-Being Research Brief 1: Who are the Children in Foster Care?* Washington DC.

American Medical Association (AMA). (1995). *Diagnostic and Treatment Guidelines on Mental Health Effects of Family Violence.* Chicago IL.

American Youth Policy Forum. (2005). *By the Numbers: Every Nine Seconds in America a Student Becomes a Dropout.* Washington DC. http://www.aypf.org/publications/EveryNineSeconds.pdf (accessed September 4, 2007).

Aspen Institute. *See* Commission on No Child Left Behind.

Bair-Merritt, M.H., Feudtner, C., Localio, R., Feinstein, J., Rubin, D, and Holmes, R. (2008). Health care use of children whose female caregivers have intimate partner violence histories. *Arch Pediatric Adolescent Medicine,* 162(2):134–139.

Baker, J. (2010). *Divorce Statistics.* Springfield, MO: Forest Institute of Professional Psychology.

Barr, R. and Parrett, W. (2003). *Saving Our Students—Saving Our Schools: 50 Proven Strategies.* Glenview, IL: Skylight Professional Development Publishing.

Beck, E.L. (1999). Prevention and intervention programming: Lessons from an after-school program. *The Urban Review,* 31(1): 107–124.

Becker, H. (2008). Alcohol dependence, withdrawal and relapse. *Neuroscience: Pathways to Alcohol Dependence Part II— Neuroadaptation,* Risk, and Recovery, 31(4).

Benson, P.L., Galbraith, J. and Espeland, P. (1988) *What Kids Need to Succeed.* Minneapolis, MN: Free Spirit.

Black, C. (1981). *It Will Never Happen to Me.* New York: Ballantine Books.

Blake, W. (1790). *The Marriage of Heaven and Hell.* Oxford, England: Oxford University Press.

Blakemore, C. (1998). *A Public School of Your Own.* Golden, CO: Adams-Pomeroy Press.

Bradshaw, J. (1988). *Bradshaw On: The Family.* Deerfield Beach, FL: Health Communications.

189

Bradshaw, J. (1988). *Healing the Shame That Binds You.* Deerfield Beach, FL: Health Communications.

Bruner, C. (1996). *Potential Returns on Investment from a Comprehensive Family Center Approach in High-Risk Neighborhoods: Background Paper, Allegheny County Study.* Des Moines, IA: Child and Family Policy Center.

Bruner, C. and Scott, S. (1994). *Investment-Based Budgeting—The Principles in Converting from a Remediation Response to a Prevention/Investment Budget. Occasional Paper #11.* Des Moines, IA: Child and Family Policy Center.

Bureau for Children, Youth and Families, Division of Community Services, Wisconsin Department of Health and Social Services. (1992). *1992 Child Abuse and Neglect Report.* Madison, WI.

Bureau of Economic Analysis, U.S. Department of Commerce. (2007). *National Income and Products Accounts (NIPS) Tables, Table 1.1.4. Price Indexes for Gross Domestic Product, 2007.*

Caldwell, R.A. (1992). *The Costs of Child Abuse vs. Child Abuse Prevention: Michigan's Experience.* East Lansing, MI: Michigan Children's Trust Fund/Michigan State University.

Carnegie Foundation for the Advancement of Teaching. (2010). Frequently asked questions. http://www.carnegiefoundation.org/faqs.

Catalano, R.F, Berglund, M.L., Ryan, J.A., Lonczak, H. and Hawkins, J. (2002). Defining and evaluating positive youth development. *Prevention & Treatment,* volume 5, article 15.

ChildHelp. (2010). Frequently asked questions. http://www.childhelp.org/pages/faq.

Children's Defense Fund. (2005). *The Children's Defense Fund's 2005 Annual Report.* Washington, DC.

Children's Defense Fund. (2010a). *The Children's Defense Fund's 2010 Annual Report.* Washington, DC.

Children's Defense Fund. (2009). *Each Day in America.* http://www.childrensdefense. org/child-research-data-publications/each-day-in-america.html.

Children's Defense Fund. (2010b). *State of America's Children 2010—Child Poverty Section.* http://www.childrensdefense.org/child-research-data-publications/state-of-americas-children-child-poverty-2010.html.

Child Welfare Information Gateway, Administration for Children and Families, U.S. Department of Health and Human Services. (2006). *Long-Term Consequences of Child Abuse and Neglect.* http://www.childwelfare.gov/pubs/factsheets/long_term_consequences .cfm (accessed January 30, 2007).

Child Welfare League of America (CWLA). (2007). *The President's FY 2008 Budget and Children.* http://www.cwla.org/advocacy/budgetchildren08.htm.

Commission on No Child Left Behind, Aspen Institute. (2009). *Background for the Commission's Hearing on Teacher and Principal Effectiveness.* http://www. aspeninstitute.org/sites/default/files/content/docs/Teacher%20Principal%20Effectiveness%20Backgrounder.pdf.

Conrath, J. (1997). *Getting Started.* Lopez Island, WA: Our Other Youth.

Conrath, J. (1994). *You, Youth, Responsibility, and Self Control.* Lopez Island, WA: Our Other Youth.

Crespi, T.D. (1995). Adult children of alcoholics: The family praxis. *Family Therapy,* 22: 81–95.

Crozier, J. and Barth, R. (2005). Cognitive and academic functioning in maltreated children. *Children & Schools,* 27(4): 197–206.

Dallmann-Jones, A. (2006). *Handbook of Effective Teaching and Assessment Strategies.* 2nd ed. Lancaster, PA: RLD Publications.

Dallmann-Jones, A. (1996). *Resolving Unfinished Business: Assessing the Effects of Being Raised in a Dysfunctional Environment.* Fond du Lac, WI: Three Blue Herons Publishing.

Dallmann-Jones, A. and Vande Zande, C. (2000). *Quality Facets of At-Risk Education Programs: The NAREN NINE.* Fond du Lac, WI: National At-Risk Education Network.

Daro, D. (1988). *Confronting Child Abuse: Research for Effective Program Design,* New York: The Free Press.

Dembo, M.H. and Eaton, M.J. (2000). Self-regulation of academic learning in middle-level schools. *The Elementary School Journal,* 100(5): 473–490.

Dicintio, M.J. and Gee, S. (1999). Control is the key: Unlocking the motivation of at-risk students. *Psychology in the Schools,* 36(3): 231–237.

Doll, B. and Hess, R.S. (2001). Through a new lens: Contemporary psychological perspectives on school completion and dropping out of high school. *School Psychology Quarterly,* 16(4): 351–356.

Dryfoos, J.G. (1997) The prevalence of problem behaviors: Implications for programs. In *Healthy Children 2010: Enhancing Children's Wellness* (pp.17–46). Thousand Oaks, CA: Sage.

Dube, S.R., Anda, R.F., Felitti, V.J., Chapman, D., Williamson, D.F. and Giles, W.H. (2001). Childhood abuse, household dysfunction and the risk of attempted suicide throughout the life span: Findings from the Adverse Childhood Experiences Study. *Journal of the American Medical Association (JAMA),* 286: 3089–3096.

Dubowitz, H. (1990). Costs and effectiveness of interventions in child maltreatment. *Child Abuse and Neglect,* 14(2): 177–186.

Dugger, C. and Desmoulin-Kherat, S. (1996). Helping younger dropouts get back into school. *Middle School Journal,* 28(November): 29–33.

Duke, D.J. and Griesdorn, J. (1999). Considerations in the design of alternative schools. *The Clearing House,* 73(2): 89–92.

English, D.J., Widom, C.S. and Brandford, C. (2004). Another look at the effects of child abuse. *National Institute of Justice (NIJ) Journal,* 251: 23–24.

Esters, I. (2003). Salient worries of at-risk youth: Needs assessment using The Things I Worry About scale. *Adolescence.* 38(150): 279–285.

Every Child Matters Education Fund Annual Report. (2003). *How Federal Budget Priorities and Tax Cuts are Harming America's Children.* Washington DC: Every Child Matters.

Farber, P. (1998). Small schools work best for disadvantaged students. *The Harvard Education Letter,* 14(2).

Farmer, S. (1989). *Adult Children of Abusive Parents.* Los Angeles: Lowell House Legacy.

Farmer, S. (1992). *Healing Words.* New York: Ballantine.

Farmer, S. (2002). *Sacred Ceremonies.* Carlsbad, CA: Hay House.

Farmer, S. (1991). *The Wounded Male.* New York: Bantam Books.

Federal Interagency Forum on Child and Family Statistics. (2010). *America's Children in Brief: Key National Indicators of Well-Being, 2010.* http://www.childstats. gov/americaschildren/index.asp.

Finn, C. (2000). *Charter Schools in Action: Renewing Public Education.* Princeton, NJ: Princeton University Press.

Fischer, J., Wampler, R., Lyness, K. and Thomas, E. (1992). Offspring codependency: Blocking the impact of the family of origin. *Family Dynamics of Addiction Quarterly* 2: 1–12.

Franey, K., Geffner, R. and Falconer, R., (eds.). (2001). *The Cost of Child Maltreatment: Who Pays? We All Do.* San Diego, CA: Family Violence & Sexual Assault Institute.

Fromm, S. (2001). *Total Estimated Cost of Child Abuse and Neglect in the United States: Statistical Evidence.* Study report. Chicago, IL: Prevent Child Abuse America.

Gandara, P. and Chavez, L. (2000). *Putting the Cart Before the Horse: Latinos and Higher Education.* Davis and Berkeley, CA: University of California.

Geen, R., Waters, S., Tumlin, K.C. and Boots, S.W. (1999). *The Cost of Protecting Vulnerable Children: Understanding Federal, State, and Local Child Welfare Spending.* New York: The Urban Institute.

Gil, E. (1988). *Treatment of Adult Survivors of Childhood Abuse.* Fairfax, VA: Launch Press.

Goldman, J., Salus, M.K., Wolcott, D. and Kennedy, K.Y. (2003). *A Coordinated Response to Child Abuse and Neglect: The Foundation for Practice.* Child Abuse and Neglect User Manual Series. Washington, DC: U.S. Government Printing Office.

Gould, M.S. and O'Brien, T. (1995). *Child Maltreatment in Colorado: The Value of Prevention and the Cost of Failure to Prevent.* Denver, CO: Center for Human Investment Policy, University of Colorado at Denver.

Greenberg, D.F. and West, V. (2001). State prison populations and their growth. 1971–1991. *Criminology.* 39: 615–654.

Greene, J. (2002). *The GED Myth.* New York: Manhattan Institute for Public Policy Research.

Gregory, T. (2001). Fear of success? Ten ways alternative schools pull their punches. *Phi Delta Kappan,* 82(8): 577–582.

Groth, C. (1998). Dumping ground or effective alternative: Dropout-prevention programs in urban schools. *Urban Education,* 33(2): 218–242.

Grunbaum, J.A., Kann, L., Kinchen, S.A., Ross, J.G., Gowda, V.R., Collins, J.L. and Kolbe, L.J. (2000). Youth risk behavior surveillance national alternative high school youth risk behavior survey, United States, 1998. *Journal of School Health,* 70(1): 5–17.

Grunbaum, J.A., Lowry, R. and Kann, L. (2001). Prevalence of health-related behaviors among alternative high school students as compared with students attending regular high schools. *Journal of Adolescent Health,* 29(5): 337–343.

Hagele, D.M. (2005). The impact of maltreatment on the developing child. *North Carolina Medical Journal,* 66: 356–359.

Hammer, B. (2003). Charter schools produce higher test scores, but segregated environment: Recent studies assess race, academic achievement in the nation's charter schools. Manhattan Institute study. *Black Issues in Higher Education,* August 28: 4–6.

Hammerle (1992), as cited in Daro, D. (1988) *Confronting Child Abuse.* New York: The Free Press.

Haskins, R., Wulczyn, F. and Webb, M. (2007). *Child Protection: Using Research to Improve Policy and Practice.* Washington, DC: Brookings Institution Press.

Hayward, A., and DePanfilis, D. (2007) Foster children with an incarcerated parent: Predictors of reunification. *Children and Youth Services Review.* 29, 10, 1320–1334.

Henley, P., Fuston, J. and Peters, T. (2000). Rescuing elementary school troublemakers. *The Education Digest,* 65(8): 48–52.

Hill, H.M. and Jones, L.P. (1997). Children's and parents' perceptions of children's exposure to violence in urban neighborhoods. *Journal of the National Medical Association,* 89(4): 270–276.

Holloway, J.H. (2000). Extracurricular activities: The path to academic success? *Educational Leadership,* 57(4): 87–88.

Hooks, G., Mosher, C., Genter, S., Rotolo, T. and Lobao, L. (2010). Revisiting the impact of prison building on job growth: Education, incarceration, and county-level employment. 1976–2004. *Social Science Quarterly,* 91: 228-244.

Horn, L.J. and Chen, X. (1998). *Toward Resiliency: At-Risk Students Who Make It to College.* Washington, DC: U.S. Department of Education, Office of Educational Research and Improvement.

Huxley, A. (1962). *Island.* New York: Bantam Books.

Ingersoll, S. and LeBoeuf, D. (1997). Reaching out to youth out of the education (traditional) mainstream and current (alternative) school environments. *High School Journal,* 85(2): 12–23.

Kapp, D. and Breslin, B. (2001). Restorative justice in school communities. *Youth & Society,* 33(2): 249–272.

Kaye, S. (2007). Internalizing and externalizing behaviors of adolescents in kinship and foster care: Findings from the national survey of child and adolescent well-being. Dissertation. College Park, MD: University of Maryland.

Keith, N.Z. (1996). Can urban school reform and community development be joined? *Education and Urban Society,* 28(2): 237–268.

Kelley, B.T., Thornberry, T.P. and Smith, C.A. (1997). *In the Wake of Childhood Violence.* Washington, DC: National Institute of Justice.

Kellogg, T. (1990). *Broken Toys, Broken Dreams.* Amherst, MA: Brat Publishing.

Kozol, J. (1992). *Savage Inequalities: Children in America's Schools.* New York: Harper Perennial.

Lamperes, B. (1994). Empowering at-risk students to succeed. *Educational Leadership,* 52(November): 67–70.

Land, K. (2009). *The 2009 Foundation for Child Development—Child and Youth Well-Being Index (CWI) Report.* Durham, NC: Duke University.

Lange, C. (1998). Characteristics of alternative schools and programs serving at-risk students. *The High School Journal,* 81(4):183–198.

Lavin-Loucks, D. (2006). The academic achievement gap. *Williams Institute Research Brief,* July: 1–12.

LeBoeuf, D. (1997). *Reaching Out to Youth Out of The Mainstream.* Washington, DC: Office of Juvenile Justice and Delinquency Prevention, Office of Justice Programs, U.S. Department of Justice.

Leventhal, T. and Brooks-Gunn, J. (2000). The neighborhoods they live in: The effects of neighborhood residence on child and adolescent outcomes. *Psychological Bulletin,* 126(2): 309–337.

Levine, E. (2002). One kid at a time: big lessons from a small school. Series on school reform. *Phi Delta Kappan,* 72(7): 550–554.

Linton, E.P. (2000). Alternative schooling for troubled youth in rural communities. *School Administrator,* 57(2): 46.

Loeber, R. and Stouthamer-Loeber, M. (1987). Prediction. In *Handbook of Juvenile Delinquency,* edited by H.C. Quay. New York: Wiley.

Lofstrom, M. and Tyler, J. (2005). Is the GED an effective route to postsecondary education? Paper presented at the 2005 Fall Research Conference of the Association for Public Policy Analysis and Management, Washington DC, November 3–5.

MacIver, D.J., Balfanz, R. and Plank, S. (1998). *An Elective Replacement Approach to Providing Extra Help in Math—The CATAMA Program (Computer- and Team-Assisted Mathematics Acceleration).* Report Number 21. Baltimore, MD: Center for Research on Education of Students Placed At Risk.

Martínez, Y.G. and Jos A.V. (2000). *Involving Migrant Families in Education.* ERIC Clearinghouse on Rural Education and Small Schools, ERIC Digest EDORC-00-4.

Martone, C. (2005). *Loving Through Bars—Children with Parents in Prison.* Santa Monica, CA: Santa Monica Press.

Maslow, A. (1971). *The Farther Reaches of Human Nature.* New York: Viking Press.

McCarthey, S. (1999). Identifying teacher practices that connect home and school. *Education and Urban Society,* 32(1): 83–107.

McCrae, J. (2009). Emotional and behavioral problems reported in child welfare over 3 years. *Journal of Emotional and Behavioral Disorders,* 17(1): 17–28

McCrae, J. and Barth, R. (2008). Using cumulative risk to screen for mental health problems in child welfare. *Research on Social Work Practice,* 18(2): 144–159.

McGee, J. (2001). Reflections of an alternative school administrator. *Phi Delta Kappan,* 82(8): 588–592.

Melbourne, F.H., Blumberg, E.J., Liles, S., Powell, L., Morrison, T.C., Duran, G., Sipan, C.L., Burkhamd, S. and Kelley, N. (2001). Training AIDS and anger prevention social skills in at-risk adolescents. *Journal of Counseling & Development,* 79: 347–355.

Middleton-Moz, J. (1989). *Children of Trauma.* Deerfield Beach, FL: Health Communications.

Miller, A. (1998). The childhood trauma. Lecture at the Lexington 92nd Street YWCA, New York City.

Miller, A. (1981). *The Drama of the Gifted Child.* New York: Basic Books.

Miller, A. (1988). *For Your Own Good.* New York: Farrar, Straus and Giroux.

Miller, R.M., Cohen, M.A. and Wiersema, B. (1996). *Victims Cost and Consequences: A New Look.* Washington, DC: The National Institute of Justice.

Missouri Children's Trust Fund (1997). *The Economic Costs of Shaken Baby Syndrome Survivors in Missouri.* Jefferson City, MO: Missouri Children's Trust Fund.

Myers, J.E.B., Berliner, L., Briere, J. and Hendrix, C.T. (2001). *The APSAC Handbook on Child Maltreatment.* 2nd ed. Thousand Oaks, CA: Sage.

National At-Risk Education Network (NAREN). (2004). *Nine Facets of Quality At-Risk Education.* Marco Island, FL: National At-Risk Education Network.

Thakur, M. (ed.). (2002). *NYEC EDNet Tools for Transformational Education.* Washington DC: National Youth Employment Coalition.

Olds, D.L., Henderson, C.R., Phelps, C., Kitzman, H. and Hanks, C. (1993). Effect of prenatal and infancy nurse home visitation on government spending. *Medical Care,* 31(2): 155–174.

Oxley, D. (1993). *Organizing Schools into Smaller Units: A Planning Guide.* Philadelphia: National Center on Education in the Inner Cities at the Temple University Center for Research in Human Development and Education.

Paglin, C. and Fager, J. (1997). *Alternative Schools: Approaches for Students at Risk.* Portland, OR: Northwest Regional Educational Laboratory.

Panfilis, D.D. and Salus, M.K. (1991). *A Coordinated Response to Child Abuse and Neglect: A Basic Manual.* DHHS Publication No. (ACF) 92-30362. Washington DC: U.S. Department of Health and Human Services, Administration for Children and Families.

Peterson, R.L. and Smith, C.R. (2002). Dealing with behaviors perceived as unacceptable in schools: The interim alternative education program. *Addressing the Diverse Needs of Children and Youth with Emotional-Behavioral Disorders—Programs That Work.* Alexandria, VA: The Council for Children with Behavioral Disorders.

Petit, M.R. and Curtis, P. (1997). *Child Abuse and Neglect: A Look at the States.* 1997 CWLA Stat Book. Washington, DC: CWLA Press.

Pew Charitable Trust. (2009). *One in 31: The Long Reach of American Corrections.* Washington, DC: The Pew Charitable Trusts.

Plotnick, R.D. and Deppman, L. (1999). Using benefit-cost analysis to assess child abuse prevention and intervention programs. *Child Welfare,* 78(3): 381–407.

Pride Surveys (2003). *2002–2003 National Summary. PRIDE Questionnaire Report for Grades 6 thru 12.* Bowling Green, KY.

Pride Surveys. (2009). *2008–2009 National Summary. PRIDE Questionnaire Report for Grades 6 thru 12.* Bowling Green, KY.

Ravitch, D. (2000). *Left Back: A Century of Failed School Reforms.* New York: Simon & Schuster.

Renzulli, J.S. (1998). A rising tide lifts all ships: Developing the gifts and talents of all students. *Phi Delta Kappan,* 80(2): 104–111.

Reyes, O., Kobus, K. and Gillock, K. (1999). Career aspirations of urban, Mexican American adolescent females. *Hispanic Journal of Behavioral Sciences,* 21(3): 366–382.

Rivera, L. (2003). Changing women: an ethnographic study of homeless mothers and popular education. *Journal of Sociology and Social Welfare,* June: 45–60.

Rodenstein, J.M. (1990). *Children at Risk: A Resource and Planning Guide.* Madison, WI: Wisconsin Department of Public Instruction.

Rodriguez-Brown, F.V., Li, R.F. and Albom, J.B. (1999). Hispanic parents' awareness and use of literacy-rich environments at home and in the community. *Education and Urban Society,* 32(1): 41–58.

Rogers, C. R. and Freiberg, H. J. (1994). *Freedom To Learn.* 3rd ed. Columbus, OH: Prentice Hall.

Romo, H.D. (1999). *Reaching Out: Best Practices for Educating Mexican-Origin Children and Youth.* Charleston, WV: The ERIC Clearinghouse on Rural Education and Small Schools.

Sagor, R. (1999). Equity and excellence in public schools: The role of the alternative school. *The Clearing House,* 73(2), 72–76.

Sakayi, D.N.R. (2001). Intellectual indignation: Getting at the roots of student resistance in an alternative high school program. *Education,* 122(2): 414–423.

Samenow, S. (1989). *Before It's Too Late.* New York: Random House.

Sanders, M.G. (1997). Building Effective School-Family-Community Partnerships in a Large Urban School District. Baltimore, MD: Johns Hopkins University.

Sanders, M.G. and Epstein, J.L. (1998). *School-Family-Community Partnerships in Middle and High Schools: From Theory to Practice.* Report No. 22. Baltimore, MD: Center for Research on the Education of Students Placed at Risk.

Schargel, F. (2003). *Dropout Prevention Tools.* Larchmont, NY: Eye on Education.

Schargel, F. (2004). *Helping Students Graduate: A Strategic Approach to Dropout Prevention.* Larchmont, NY: Eye on Education.

Schargel, F. and Smink, J. (2001). *Strategies to Help Solve Our School Dropout Problem.* Larchmont, NY: Eye On Education.

Scheurich, J.J. (1998). Highly successful and loving, public elementary schools populated mainly by low-SES children of color. *Urban Education,* 33(4): 151–491.

Schwartz, W. (2001). *Strategies for Improving the Educational Outcomes of Latinas.* New York: ERIC Clearinghouse on Urban Education.

Schwartz, R.B., Wurtzel, J. and Olson, L. (2007). Attracting and retaining teachers. *OECD Observer,* number 261(May): 27–28.

Sedgley, N.H., Scott, C.E., Williams, N.A. and Derrick, F.W. (2010). Prison's dilemma: Do education and jobs programs affect recidivism? *Economica,* 77: 497–517.

Sedlak, A. and Broadhurst, D. (1996). *The Third National Incidence Study of Child Abuse and Neglect: NIS 3.* Washington, DC: U.S. Department of Health and Human Services.

Seixas, J.S., and Youcha, G. (1985). *Children of Alcoholics: A Survivor's Manual.* New York: Crown Publishers.

Slavin, R.E. and Fashola, O.S. (1998). *Show Me the Evidence! Proven and Promising Programs for America's Schools.* Thousand Oaks, CA: Corwin Press.

Sloan Work and Family Research Network. (2010). *Public Policy Platform on Flexible Work Arrangements.* http://workplaceflexibility2010.org/images/uploads/reports/report_1.pdf.

Smith, A. (1988.) *Grandchildren of Alcoholics.* Deerfield Beach, FL: Health Communications.

Smith, S. and Thomases, J. (2001). *CBO Schools: Profiles in Transformational Education.* Washington, DC: AED Center for Youth Development and Policy Research.

Spelman, W. (2009). Crime, cash, and limited options: Explaining the prison boom. *Criminology & Public Policy,* 8: 29–77.

Spring, J. (2001). *Deculturalization and the Struggle for Equality: A Brief History of the Education of Dominated Cultures in the United States.* Boston: McGraw-Hill.

Spring, J. (2000). *The Universal Right to Education: Justification, Definition, and Guidelines.* Mahwah, NJ: Lawrence Erlbaum Associates.

Springer, K.W., Sheridan, J., Kuo, D. and Carnes, M. (2007). Long-term physical and mental health consequences of childhood physical abuse: Results from a large population-based sample of men and women. *Child Abuse & Neglect,* 31: 517–530.

Steinglass, P. (1987). *The Alcoholic Family.* New York: Basic Books.

Stillwell, R. (2009). *Public School Graduates and Dropouts from the Common Core of Data: School Year 2006–07 (NCES 2010-313).* Washington, DC: National Center for Education Statistics, Institute of Education Sciences, U.S. Department of Education. http://nces.ed.gov/ pubsearch/pubsinfo.asp?pubid=2010313 (accessed June 1, 2010).

Swan, N. (1998). Exploring the role of child abuse on later drug abuse: Researchers face broad gaps in information. *NIDA Notes,* 13(2). http://www.nida.nih.gov/NIDA_Notes/NNVol13N2/exploring.html (accessed April 27, 2006).

Teicher, M.D. (2000). Wounds that time won't heal: The neurobiology of child abuse. *Cerebrum: The Dana Forum on Brain Science,* 2(4): 50–67.

Tharp, R. and Gallimore, R. (1988). *Rousing Minds to Life: Teaching, Learning and Schooling in Social Context.* New York: Cambridge University Press.

Tobin, T. and Sprague, J. (2000). Alternative education strategies: reducing violence in school and the community. *Journal of Emotional & Behavioral Disorders,* 8(3): 177–187.

University of Wisconsin-Madison. (2010). Price of prison for children. *Science Daily,* August 9, 2010. http://www.sciencedaily.com/releases/2010/08/100809142050.htm.

U.S. Bureau of the Census. (2000). *Census 2000.* http://www.census.gov/main/www/cen2000.html.

U.S. Bureau of the Census. (2008). *Current Population Survey: Annual Social and Economic Supplements.* Washington DC.

U.S. Bureau of the Census. (2009). *Custodial Mothers and Fathers and Their Child Support: 2007* by Timothy S. Grall. http://www.census.gov/prod/2009pubs/p60–237.pdf.

U.S. Department of Commerce. (2010). Census Bureau: Current Population Survey. U.S. Department of Education: National Center for Education Statistics: Annual Social and Economic Supplement.

U.S. Department of Health and Human Services. (2008). *Child Maltreatment 2006.* Washington, DC: U.S. Government Printing Office.

U.S. Department of Health and Human Services. (1999). *Mental Health: A Report of the Surgeon General.* Rockville, MD.

U.S. Department of Justice. (2008). *Federal Prison System Buildings and Facilities.* Washington DC. http://www.justice.gov/jmd/2008justification/pdf/37_bop_bf.pdf.

U.S. General Accounting Office Publication. (1992). *Child Abuse: Prevention Programs Need Greater Emphasis.* Publication. Report Number: HRD-92-99. Washington DC: U.S. Government Printing Office.

U.S. General Accounting Office Publication. (2002). *School Dropouts. Education Could Play a Stronger Role in Identifying and Disseminating Promising Prevention Strategies.* Publication GAO-02-240. Washington DC: U.S. Government Printing Office.

Walls, R., Nardi, A., von Minden, A. and Hoffman N. (2002). The characteristics of effective and ineffective teachers. *Teacher Education Quarterly,* 29(1): 39–48.

Wang, C. and Holton, J. (2007). *Total Estimated Cost of Child Abuse and Neglect in the United States.* Chicago: Prevent Child Abuse America.

Watts-English, T., Fortson, B.L., Gibler, N., Hooper, S.R. and De Bellis, M. (2006). The psychobiology of maltreatment in childhood. *Journal of Social Sciences,* 62(4): 717–736.

Wegscheider-Cruse, S. (1989). *Another Chance: Hope and Health for the Alcoholic Family.* Palo Alto, CA: Science and Behavior Books.

Wehlage, G., Rutter, R., Smith, G., Lesko, N. and Fernandez, R. (1989). *Reducing the Risk: Schools as Communities of Support.* Philadelphia, PA: The Falmer Press.

Weiner, L., Leighton, M. and Funkhouser, J. (2009). *Helping Hispanic Students Reach High Academic Standards: An Idea Book.* Washington, DC: U.S. Dept. of Education, Office of Educational Research and Improvement, Educational Resources Information Center.

Weissberg, R.P., Walberg, H.J., O'Brien, M.U. and Kuster, C.B. (eds.). (2003). *Long-Term Trends in the Well-Being of Children and Youth.* Washington, DC: Child Welfare League of America Press.

Whitfield, C. (1991). *Co-Dependence: Healing The Human Condition.* Deerfield Beach, FL: Health Communications.

Whitfield, C. (1990). *A Gift To Myself.* Deerfield Beach, FL: Health Communications.

Whitfield, C. (1984). *Healing the Child Within.* Deerfield Beach, FL: Health Communications.

Wiest, D.J., Wong, E.H., Cervantes, J.M., Craik, L. and Kreil, D.A. (2001). Intrinsic motivation among regular, special, and alternative education high school students. *Adolescence,* 36(141): 111–126.

Woititz, J. (1987). *Adult Children of Alcoholics.* Deerfield Beach, FL: Health Communications.

Woititz, J. (1989). *Healing your Sexual Self.* Deerfield Beach, FL: Health Communications.

Woititz, J. (1994).Workshop, Holiday Inn, Madison, WI.

Zolotor, A., Kotch, J., Dufort, V., Winsor, J., Catellier, D. and Bou-Saada, I. (1999). School performance in a longitudinal cohort of children at risk of maltreatment. *Maternal and Child Health Journal,* 3(1): 19–27

Index

About the Author

Anthony Dallmann-Jones, PhD, founder and director of the National At-Risk Education Network (NAREN), has been a well-known advocate for at-risk youth and their educators for many years. He discovered the absence of an effective voice, and organized a support system to address perspectives on the critical issues in at-risk education that both students and educators must face on a daily basis. Society and its school systems generally appear to be in denial or confused and frustrated as to the best action steps to take. Meanwhile, the at-risk youth and the educators who care about them are frequently misunderstood and isolated. It is from these roots that Dr. Dallmann-Jones formed his ARME (or "At-Risk Mindful Educator") website and newsgroup in 1997. From these roots NAREN came to fruition as a 501(c)(3) non-profit corporation on January 1, 2001.

Dr. Dallmann-Jones, a graduate of Florida State University, was born into poverty in Mobile, Alabama, and has experienced firsthand the impact of being raised in a dysfunctional family. He began teaching in 1965 in a small rural town in Ohio. Since then he has taught in middle schools, high schools, colleges, and medium-security prisons. He was a central office educational administrator in Jacksonville, Florida, and a Title III project director on Lookout Mountain, Tennessee.

Dr. Dallmann-Jones helped design the first accredited master's degree program in alternative education specializing in working with at-risk youth in the United States. His classes are taught online through Marian University's DIAL Program (Differentiated Instruction for Alternative Learning). He has worked on behalf of at-risk "street children" with the Police Athletic League, in halfway houses, as a psychotherapist, and on three Native American reservations.

Dr. Dallmann-Jones has published several books, including:

- Resolving Unfinished Business: Assessing the Effects of Being Raised in a Dysfunctional Environment
- The Expert Educator: A Reference Manual of Teaching Strategies for Quality Education
- The Handbook of Effective Teaching and Assessment Strategies
- Teaching Problem-Solving: Primary Domino Thinking
- Educating for Human Greatness (with Lynn Stoddard)

Dr. Dallmann-Jones is currently a graduate professor of educational psychology at Marian University. He speaks nationwide in schools, to civic groups, and at conventions on both at-risk education topics and teacher rejuvenation issues. He has spoken nationally and internationally (most recently in Moscow and Singapore) about the plight of at-risk youth in our world.

Contact Dr. Dallmann-Jones:
Anthony Dallmann-Jones, PhD
440 Seaview Court—Suite 1911
Marco Island, FL 34145
E-mail: director@naren.info

Products

Assessment Forms

Classification System for Child Abuse & Neglect (CSCAN)

Each sheet includes all current CSCAN categories in a checklist format. A Master CSCAN is personalized for each customer. The Masters may be reproduced in-house for the use of the agency or school, but not for the entire school district. Each Master is imprinted with the name and address of a particular school and may not be used outside that school (or agency) address. (6 pages)

Early Assessment of At-Risk Behaviors in Children

EAARB is a research-based and field-tested preliminary assessment for classroom teachers in determining if pre-school/primary children are potentially at-risk of not succeeding in school and/or life. It is concise and clear and will help clarify and document for the record what teachers observe as potentially harmful influences in a child's life. To be clear, it provides leverage—a paper trail of proof that the teacher has done the right thing, the professionally proper thing, for a child who apparently needs special attention. The EAARB is sold and licensed with the printed name of the individual school (not the school district) and can be reprinted and used in that school (only) for the life of the school. Once ordered you will be contacted by email for the name of the school. (3 pages)

Assessment of At-Risk Behaviors in Middle School

AARBMS is a research-based and field-tested mid-kid assessment for classroom teachers in determining if middle school children are potentially at-risk of not succeeding in school and/or life. It is concise and clear and will assist in clarifying and documenting what teachers observe as potentially harmful influences in a child's life. To be clear, it provides leverage—a paper trail of proof that the teacher has done the right thing, the professionally proper thing, for a child who apparently needs special attention.

The AARBMS is sold and licensed with the printed name of the individual school (not the school district) and can be reprinted and used in that school (only) for the life of the school. Once ordered you will be contacted by email for the name of the school. (3 pages)

The NAREN Self-Study Kit

The NAREN Nine Facets of Quality At-Risk Education

The NAREN Self-Study Kit assists schools or school systems achieve an in-depth look at how they can better meet the needs of at-risk youth by:

1. Assessing their current at-risk program against quality education standards developed by NAREN
2. Reforming their existing at-risk education program with effective guidelines
3. Utilizing the guidelines in developing new at-risk education programs
4. Preparing for certification by NAREN reviewer(s)

Included in the NAREN Self-Study Kit is a guideline manual and a workbook with all nine NAREN standards, indicators of compliance, benchmark evidence suggestions, and spaces to notate locations of authentic evidence in the portfolio to be submitted for review. Also included are full instructions for applying for certification, application forms, suggested timetables, and contact information. (140 pages)

Order Form

Name: _____ Tel. _____

Address: _____

City & State _____ Zip _____

E-mail (please print) _____

__ CSCAN Assessment Masters   only $3 s/h   ____

__ National At-Risk Education Network Self-Study Kit $9.95 + $5 s/h   ____

__ Early Assessment of At-Risk Behaviors (Elem.School) $46.95 + $3 s/h   ____

__ Assessment of At-Risk Behaviors in Middle School $46.95 + $3 s/h   ____

__ Angels & Warriors T-shirt $19.95 + $3 s/h   ____

__ Educating for Human Greatness $14.95 + $3 s/h   ____

Note: If you order 2 or more items by purchase order, money order, or check the total shipping/handling is $5

TOTAL: _____

Allow 3 weeks for delivery. Satisfaction guaranteed for amount of purchase.

Mail order form along with check/money or purchase order #_____ to:

National At-Risk Education Network
440 Seaview Court, #1911
Marco Island, FL 34145
920-251-2052

You may fax Purchase Orders to: 888-678-4902

Credit Card Holders:
Place secure credit card orders online at the NAREN website,
www.AtRiskEducation.net.